Managing Healthcare Ethically

Managing Healthcare Ethically

THIRD EDITION

VOLUME 1

Leadership Roles *and* Responsibilities

ACHE Management Series

William A. Nelson | Paul B. Hofmann | Editors

Your board, staff, or clients may also benefit from this book's insight. For information on quantity discounts, contact the Health Administration Press Marketing Manager at (312) 424-9450.

26 25 24 23 22 5 4 3 2 1

Library of Congress Cataloging-in-Publication Data

Names: Nelson, William A., editor. | Hofmann, Paul B., 1941– editor.

Title: Managing healthcare ethically / William A. Nelson, Paul B. Hofmann, editors.

Other titles: Management series (Ann Arbor, Mich.)

Description: Third edition. | Chicago, IL : Health Administration Press, [2022] | Series: HAP/ACHE management series | Includes bibliographical references. | Contents: v. 1. Leadership roles and responsibilities — v. 2. Organizational concerns — v. 3. Clinical challenges. | Summary: "This book discusses the numerous and complex issues that healthcare executives encounter every day as an intrinsic part of organizational life"— Provided by publisher.

Identifiers: LCCN 2021023677 (print) | LCCN 2021023678 (ebook) | ISBN 9781640552500 (v. 1 ; paperback ; alk. paper) | ISBN 9781640552555 (v. 2 ; paperback ; alk. paper) | ISBN 9781640552609 (v. 3 ; paperback ; alk. paper) | ISBN 9781640552470 (v. 1 ; epub) | ISBN 9781640552487 (v. 1 ; mobi) | ISBN 9781640552524 (v. 2 ; epub) | ISBN 9781640552531 (v. 2 ; mobi) | ISBN 9781640552579 (v. 3 ; epub) | ISBN 9781640552586 (v. 3 ; mobi)

Subjects: MESH: Health Services Administration—ethics | Leadership

Classification: LCC RA971 (print) | LCC RA971 (ebook) | NLM W 84.1 | DDC 362.1068—dc23

LC record available at https://lccn.loc.gov/2021023677

LC ebook record available at https://lccn.loc.gov/2021023678

The paper used in this publication meets the minimum requirements of American National Standard for Information Sciences—Permanence of Paper for Printed Library Materials, ANSI Z39.48-1984. ♾™

Acquisitions editor: Jennette McClain; Project manager: Andrew Baumann; Cover designer: Book Buddy Media; Layout: Integra

Found an error or a typo? We want to know! Please e-mail it to hapbooks@ache.org, mentioning the book's title and putting "Book Error" in the subject line.

For photocopying and copyright information, please contact Copyright Clearance Center at www.copyright.com or at (978) 750-8400.

Health Administration Press
A division of the Foundation of the American
College of Healthcare Executives
300 S. Riverside Plaza, Suite 1900
Chicago, IL 60606-6698
(312) 424-2800

Contents

Foreword

Our profession is one of constant change. As such, healthcare leaders are continually tasked with navigating the challenges and opportunities that surface along the way. While members of any profession are tested by their ability to navigate change while remaining resolute in their values, as healthcare executives, we are called to an even higher standard.

For that reason, ethics and ethical behavior have been a pillar of the American College of Healthcare Executives since its inception. One essential resource for our organization, our members and our profession is our *Code of Ethics*. The *Code* has been part of ACHE's fabric for more than 85 years, uniting healthcare leaders in their ethical principles and approach. Another key resource is the "Healthcare Management Ethics" column in *Healthcare Executive*, ACHE's official magazine. Since this column became a part of the magazine in 1992, it has helped ACHE members tackle the many ethical issues that can arise in our profession.

The editors of this new edition, William A. Nelson, PhD, HFACHE, and Paul B. Hofmann, DrPH, LFACHE, have regularly contributed to the column for more than 20 years and are recognized experts in healthcare management ethics. In this first volume of *Managing Healthcare Ethically*, they chose columns that focus on the ethical dilemmas that healthcare leaders regularly face *as individuals*. Ethical ambiguities are an inevitable part of healthcare, and how you address them is a reflection of your own moral compass. As such, the ability to enhance your own ethical practice and leadership benefits not only you but your organization and those in your care.

I have personally known Bill and Paul for many years and am familiar with their great work in the field of healthcare management ethics. I am grateful for their adept curation in this new edition. Their wisdom, along with that of the other column contributors, has served as an indispensable source of guidance for ACHE members and healthcare leaders across the spectrum.

As you practice leadership that embodies a system of ethics and values that puts the patient at the center of all you do, know that ACHE is here to support you and your work. While many things in healthcare are changing, one thing is not: Our commitment to stand for the voices and issues that define our profession and advance health for all.

Deborah J. Bowen, FACHE, CAE
President and CEO
American College of Healthcare Executives

Acknowledgments

We want to express our appreciation to the many authors who have contributed to this book. Their efforts were essential to this edition, as they were to the two previous editions published by Health Administration Press in 2001 and 2010.

We also want to acknowledge the editors of the American College of Healthcare Executive (ACHE) publications that continue to publish articles on ethical topics. These articles are as vital to the leaders of today's healthcare organizations as they are to the educators preparing the leaders of tomorrow.

We would like to express our sincere gratitude to the Health Administration Press team, in particular Jennette McClain for her ongoing encouragement and support throughout the process of publishing this book and Andrew Baumann for his editing assistance.

Finally, we thank Deborah J. Bowen, FACHE, CAE, president and CEO of ACHE, for her unwavering commitment and leadership in supporting the essential role of ethics in the delivery of healthcare and in the education of healthcare executives.

Introduction

THE NUMEROUS AND COMPLEX issues that healthcare executives encounter every day are an intrinsic part of organizational life. Many of these issues have significant ethical dimensions. The three separate volumes that constitute the third edition of *Managing Healthcare Ethically* build on the two previous editions. The present book, *Leadership Roles and Responsibilities*, is the first of these three volumes. The second volume focuses on organizational ethics, management, and policies, while the third volume addresses ethical challenges related to clinical care.

Each of the three volumes gathers selected columns originally written for American College of Healthcare Executives (ACHE) publications between 2010 and 2020, along with a few earlier columns that remain as appropriate today as when they were originally published. The columns were selected because of their relevance to today's healthcare environment and challenges, as well as their practical application for healthcare leaders committed to maintaining an ethically grounded organization.

In each of the three volumes that make up the third edition, we pose some provocative questions and offer other material useful for teaching purposes. Following each column, we provide two discussion questions related to the column that can be used to foster a discussion with colleagues or healthcare management students. Each volume also contains an extensive bibliography of books and articles for readers who wish to pursue particular subtopics.

Because healthcare executives play such a key role in leading ethical organizations, this first volume focuses on this crucial topic. It contains columns that highlight the myriad issues healthcare leaders encounter in ensuring ethical performance in both their institutions and the communities they serve. In this volume, we have collected columns that provide specific guidelines to expand skill sets, emphasize the relevance of personal attributes and character, and underscore the importance of maintaining an ethical culture. The content in this volume addresses the need for strong moral leadership and professionalism in guiding an organization to be ethically aligned with the organization's mission and values.

We know high-reliability healthcare organizations are managed by executives who adopt best practices that ensure the provision of value-based and high-quality patient care, have clear performance indicators, and exemplify the professional values they expect of others. As a number of the authors in this volume emphasize, senior executives are expected to establish and maintain an organizational culture that consistently promotes patient-centered care and persistently mitigates potential staff burnout.

The likelihood of conflict, daunting dilemmas, and inevitable management mistakes requires executives to be candid in their communications with governing bodies, physicians, employees, and the community. Executives must be personally resilient to cope successfully with the challenges associated with making judicious compromises, preventing staff abuse, and meeting the needs of the underserved.

A strong ethical foundation is indispensable if executives are to make sound judgments under stressful circumstances. Taking timely action when a subordinate or physician underperforms, confronting a clinician staffing shortage, and reducing a workforce when required are just a few examples of such situations.

Two vital steps increase the probability of success. One is asking the right questions when making a hiring decision, to ensure a candidate's values are aligned with those of the organization and the management team. The other is taking your ethical pulse periodically by completing ACHE's Ethics Self-Assessment (www.ache.org/about-ache/our-story/our-commitments/ethics/ethics-self-assessment). The first section of this self-assessment addresses a variety of major areas related to leadership. The second section covers relationships with significant constituencies, including the community; patients and their families; the board; colleagues and staff; clinicians; and buyers, payers, and suppliers. Some executives have benefited by having their staff complete the assessment on them as part of a 360-degree performance review.

Our goal in producing the third edition of *Managing Healthcare Ethically* is to continue raising an appreciation for how and why ethical reasoning and professionalism affect your organization's performance and success, as well as your own. We hope healthcare executives and health administration educators will use the book to reinforce the concept that ethical leadership, sensitivity, and engagement are not the sole purview of an organization's ethics committee. Instead, ethical reflection should be an inherent element in daily decision-making processes and relationships.

Instructor Resources

This book's instructor resources include PowerPoint slides, case studies, and lists of selected ethics center websites and selected ethics journals.

For the most up-to-date information about this book and its instructor resources, go to ache.org/HAP and browse for the book's title, author name, or order code (24371).

This book's instructor resources are available to instructors who adopt this book for use in their course. For access information, please e-mail hapbooks@ache.org.

The Ethics of Evidence-Based Management

Paul B. Hofmann, DrPH, LFACHE

THE ADVANTAGES OF EVIDENCE-BASED medicine have been demonstrated repeatedly. Indisputably, the adoption of clinical guidelines, pathways and protocols has contributed to improved clinical outcomes. Could the development and application of evidence-based management practices have a comparable benefit for patients, staff and, ultimately, healthcare organizations and their communities?

The succinct answer is yes, absolutely. Unfortunately, the slow and uneven adoption of best management practices is not recognized as an ethical issue. When economic resources are insufficient to acquire new technology, employ additional staff and expand or even maintain existing programs, the importance of using evidence-based management cannot be over-emphasized.

Failing to adopt documented best practices is ethically indefensible. We have an inherent fiduciary and moral responsibility to energetically pursue and implement improved management tools and techniques.

REASONS FOR SLOW ADOPTION OF BEST-DEMONSTRATED PRACTICES

There are a variety of reasons why leaders may not move quickly to replicate highly successful management practices. Four come to mind. First, some executives believe they are well experienced, know how to manage properly and do not need to invest time and effort to examine how others may be more successful in managing their organizations. They would not consider themselves to be egotistical or arrogant but, rather, confident that internal resources are sufficient to maintain continued improvement.

Second, other leaders not only are convinced they know most of the keys to effective management, but they also contend that, unlike medicine, which is primarily based on objective scientific findings, management is more of an art. Therefore, these executives view evidence-based management as an attractive academic concept but one whose value is relatively unproven.

Third, another group of executives do not feel compelled to make adoption of evidence-based management practices a high priority because the incentives for doing so are not obvious. The governing body has not expressed any concern about current practices, medical staff members continue to support the executive team and the organization is well respected by its community.

Fourth, many executives believe they simply do not have time to acquire and review potentially useful information concerning best-demonstrated management practices. These executives acknowledge the benefits of replicating best practices, but they feel overextended by confronting a seemingly unending number of crises and instead decide to delay action.

TAKING A PRAGMATIC APPROACH

The case for evidence-based management must be made more persuasively. We need to think systematically and creatively about how management best practices can be more rapidly and effectively promoted, disseminated and implemented. For example, we know many institutions have won significant state and national awards for superior performance in a wide variety of areas, including:

- Improving patient safety
- Preventing and minimizing never events
- Decreasing healthcare-acquired infections
- Making care more timely and patient centered
- Increasing patient satisfaction
- Minimizing employee turnover and absenteeism
- Reducing the cost of services
- Maximizing the value of information technology
- Promoting accountability and transparency
- Creating a learning culture
- Improving community health status
- Reducing healthcare disparities
- Demonstrating community benefit

We also know there will be more hospitals recognized for their success in:

- Lowering re-admission rates within 30 days of discharge
- Adopting electronic health records
- Expanding the cost-effective use of telemedicine
- Reducing energy consumption

Undoubtedly, many of the institutions that have won the Malcolm Baldrige National Quality Award, the American Hospital Association-McKesson Quest for Quality Prize, the Thomson Reuters 100 Top Hospitals Performance Improvement Leaders award and similar honors are led by CEOs who learned from their peers. Consequently, these same executives are almost always interested in sharing their lessons with others. The key point is that right now in each of the above areas there are reliable management policies, programs and practices that are contributing to irrefutable improvements in organizational outcomes.

TIMELY AND INFORMATIVE RESOURCES

In addition to learning from successful organizations, a growing number of recent publications contain valuable insights regarding verified means and methods for achieving exceptional progress. Five of these are particularly noteworthy.

- *Evidence-Based Management in Healthcare* by Anthony R. Kovner, PhD, David J. Fine, PhD, FACHE, and Richard D'Aquila, FACHE (Health Administration Press, 2009). The book explains how healthcare leaders can move from making educated guesses to using the best available information to make decisions.
- *Journey to Excellence: How Baldrige Health Care Leaders Succeed* by Kathleen J. Goonan, MD, Joseph A. Muzikowski and Patricia K. Stoltz (ASQ Quality Press, 2009). The book describes how nine Baldrige Award healthcare winners approached their Baldrige journey and what other healthcare leaders should do to accomplish similar benefits.
- *What Top-Performing Healthcare Organizations Know: 7 Proven Steps for Accelerating and Achieving Change* by Greg Butler and Chip Caldwell, FACHE (Health Administration Press, 2008). The authors researched more than 220 healthcare organizations to determine what differentiates high performers from organizations that fail to achieve lasting operational success.
- *Hospitals in Pursuit of Excellence [HPOE]: A Guide to Superior Performance Improvement* (American Hospital Association, 2009). This guide comprises 28 case studies of hospitals that have made significant strides in one of AHA's four initial HPOE focus areas: healthcare-acquired infections, medication management, patient throughput and patient safety. The guide is available on CD, and the

print version was mailed to every hospital in the United States in 2009.

- *Better: A Surgeon's Notes on Performance* (Metropolitan Books, 2007). Written by the remarkable surgeon and acclaimed author Atul Gawande, MD, this book is both eloquent and inspiring. Gawande notes, "Better is possible. It does not take genius. It takes diligence. It takes moral clarity. It takes ingenuity. And above all, it takes a willingness to try."

ACCELERATING THE ADOPTION OF EVIDENCE-BASED MANAGEMENT

Hospitals and other healthcare organizations have a solid track record regarding the implementation of clinical pathways, guidelines and protocols. Similarly, our most effective executives have been successful in replicating exemplary management practices through learning collaboratives and by developing innovative programs on their own. Nonetheless, we still can and should do more to close the too-large gap between the best performing institutions and those that rationalize they don't have the intellectual or financial resources to make more rapid progress.

As the public becomes better informed about the number and magnitude of problems afflicting the healthcare field, citizens legitimately will question why healthcare providers have not implemented well-documented management best practices as quickly as clinical best practices. It will be difficult to defend the status quo on an ethical basis because it cannot and should not be done.

But discomfort about being criticized is not a sufficient or compelling reason to employ evidence-based management. The motivation should be to create and sustain more effective organizations that are better able to serve our communities.

Originally published in the January/February 2010 issue of *Healthcare Executive* magazine.

Discussion Questions

Briefly describe how using evidence-based management can foster the ethical alignment of a healthcare organization.

The author identified some metrics contributing to evidence-based management. Are there additional metrics that can contribute to understanding institutional performance?

The Ethical Basis for Creating ACOs

William A. Nelson, PhD, HFACHE
and Eric Wadsworth, PhD

THERE IS WIDESPREAD RECOGNITION that healthcare organizations must focus on providing quality care and improving patient safety while at the same time addressing financial challenges through cost effectiveness. In addition to looking to government healthcare reform to address financial difficulties, healthcare executives and clinicians also have an ethical responsibility to examine their own roles and responsibilities in addressing these challenges.

The construct of the accountable care organization (ACO) has emerged in response to the need to improve patient care quality while simultaneously capturing and distributing the cost savings achieved as healthcare organizations become more efficient—often referred to as bending the value curve in healthcare. In a January/February 2007 *Health Affairs* article, Elliott Fisher and colleagues wrote: "The underlying goal of these efforts is to improve the quality and lower the costs of care by fostering greater accountability on the part of providers for their performance."

Care delivery organizations at the vanguard of this era of healthcare reform must accept the responsibility of measuring value and ensuring accountability to their patients, employees and the communities they serve. Effectively implementing patient-shared decision making and patient-centered care models and assessing variations in clinical practice patterns to inform care design will accelerate this transition. Successful ACOs should become the trusted brand in care delivery.

During a recent presentation we gave to a group of administrative and clinician leaders highlighting one component of ACOs—addressing unwarranted variations in healthcare practices—an important issue was raised. When discussing various approaches to identifying and modifying the use of certain diagnostic procedures linked to unwarranted variations, it was noted that decreasing unnecessary medical procedures may decrease revenue; therefore, decreasing unwarranted variation could actually *increase* financial losses for the organization.

As the discussion unfolded, a department chair rose and spoke. He indicated that although it might be true that there will be a negative financial fallout from decreasing the number of unnecessary procedures, "it was the right thing to do." He went on to emphasize: "Don't we have a moral responsibility to provide only clearly beneficial tests and care, and doesn't that trump everything else?"

The department chair's comment, echoed by others, illuminates the need for a science-based delivery of healthcare through an ACO approach that is grounded on an ethical foundation. Three fundamental ethics concepts underpin the moral imperative for healthcare organizations to deliver cost-effective, high-quality and safe healthcare: promoting patients' best interests through effective and safe treatment, respecting patients' values through shared decision making, and ensuring justice through stewardship of healthcare resources.

EFFECTIVE AND SAFE TREATMENT

The ethical principles of beneficence and nonmaleficence require healthcare organizations to promote the patient's best interest while decreasing potential harms or risks. This drives the need for the delivery of evidence-based healthcare. Clinicians should be offering and providing treatment and diagnostic procedures that have been scientifically assessed as effective and beneficial. Despite considerable available information regarding effective care, however, many healthcare organizations fail to deliver and monitor the use of effective care, potentially undermining actions to promote patients' best interests.

ACOs foster the moral requirement of pursuing patients' best interests by ensuring that scientifically documented effective care (flu shots, aspirin at admission for acute myocardial infarction, etc.) is delivered 100 percent of the time.

Adherence to the principles of beneficence and nonmaleficence necessitates thc need to systematically identify untested interventions and assess medical errors and propagate quality improvement approaches to avoid harming patients. In addition to monitoring care to ensure only effective care is provided, ACOs assess the care delivery system to ensure best-practice care is efficiently delivered in a timely and consistent manner to patients who are hospitalized or receiving care in outpatient settings.

SHARED DECISION MAKING

Respect for autonomy is directly linked to attaining the patient's best interest. Because only a patient will know specifically what is in his or her best interest, clinicians should promote patient self-determination by adequately taking into account patient preferences.

When offering preference-sensitive care, the provider needs to offer truthful, objective information regarding diagnostic procedures and treatment protocols. Because some treatments have significant trade-offs, patients must fully appreciate and understand the risks and benefits of their options prior to making decisions about their care. The best vehicle for promoting patient autonomy, within the context of the patient–provider relationship, is through a shared decision-making process.

Unfortunately, current patient–provider communications often fail to adequately inform patients of certain treatment options when the value is less clear, such as new, invasive and elective treatments. Research suggests modern healthcare systems sometimes take end-of-life treatment decisions out of the hands of patients and families, providing extraordinarily expensive, high-tech medicine that overrides patient preferences without adding value. ACOs foster respect for patient self-determination with a consistent, system-oriented approach, using decision aids that maximize the sharing of information about treatment options to support the communication between patients and providers.

STEWARDSHIP OF HEALTHCARE RESOURCES

Cost effectiveness is an ethical issue requiring healthcare organizations to use resources in a fair and just manner. When a patient fails to benefit after we spend healthcare dollars on ineffective care, we foster both economic and ethical failings.

In a September/October 2009 *Health Affairs* article, Norman Daniels and colleagues argue that providing care with little benefit per unit cost negates social justice by reducing resources that could be used to purchase beneficial care elsewhere. ACOs seek to decrease ineffective, unnecessary or unwanted care through performance monitoring, enabling healthcare resources to be available for more beneficial use elsewhere, such as expanded access to evidenced-based primary and preventive care.

As Daniels and colleagues point out, stewardship of resources is about setting priorities in a way that promotes value for money and is fair to all. Because social justice requires efficiency in the delivery of effective care, distributive justice requires an appropriate process to allocate resources—one that is fair, just and transparent.

Healthcare executives need to see their organizations as moral agents where services are manifest within an ethical framework with three overlapping and interconnected concepts: promoting the patient's best interest, respecting the patient's values and fostering justice. When addressing organizational financial challenges and questions of quality and safety, healthcare leadership should view the transformation into an ACO—and thus providing quality, safe and financially secure healthcare—as fulfillment of an ethical responsibility.

In the March/April issue of *Healthcare Executive*, Peter Fine, FACHE, president and CEO of Banner Health in Phoenix, described this transformation as: "moving the organizational mind-set from being a healthcare delivery company to a clinical quality company." As that happens customers will take note.

Patients and families will recognize that ACOs provide the right care, at the right time, all the time. These ethical organizations will become the trusted source for healthcare throughout their respective regions and the national models for healthcare reform.

Originally published in the July/August 2010 issue of *Healthcare Executive* magazine.

Discussion Questions

The authors indicate that an ACO healthcare delivery model seeks to enhance quality patient care and lower the costs of care. What are the barriers for achieving such a goal?

Does an ACO model of healthcare create a different form of conflicts of interest than the conflicts of interest in a traditional fee-for-service delivery model?

Addressing Racial and Ethnic Disparities in Healthcare

Paul B. Hofmann, DrPH, LFACHE

RACIAL AND ETHNIC DISPARITIES in healthcare status and access have been extensively documented.

Black women in Washington, D.C., suffer from obesity, diabetes, heart disease and generally poor health in alarmingly high numbers, and white women do not, according to a study released by the Kaiser Family Foundation. The study reveals there is a large disparity in the incidence of certain chronic diseases between black and white women. Kaiser's analysis was based on data compiled by the Centers for Disease Control and Prevention and the federal Current Population Survey from 2004 to 2006.

A study by researchers at Johns Hopkins School of Public Health and the University of Maryland found that eliminating health disparities for Asians, blacks and Latinos would have saved an estimated $229 billion in U.S. medical care expenditures between 2002 and 2006.

The racial gap in colon cancer death rates is widening. Colon and rectal cancer death rates are now nearly 50 percent higher in blacks than in whites, according to American Cancer Society research. In its 2008 report, experts partly attributed the gap to blacks' lower screening rates and poor access to quality care. Not surprisingly, research has found that minority populations have a higher level of mistrust of healthcare providers due to these inequities. Fortunately, more hospitals and other institutional providers are now becoming increasingly aware that activism, not passive behavior, is essential to achieve significant improvements.

Historically, healthcare executives have rationalized their too modest efforts in this area. Typically, disparity issues were not viewed as critical to the organization's mission; higher priorities demanded attention; and public hospitals and faith-based institutions were expected to assume principal responsibility for the provision of services to the underserved, a disproportionate number of whom are minorities. Furthermore, even in so-called progressive communities, physicians of color were not recruited or welcomed a few decades ago, and most governing boards remain predominantly white.

THREE EXEMPLARY PROGRAMS

Beginning last year, Detroit's Henry Ford Health System initiated a three-year Healthcare Equity Campaign to address potential sources of inequality in healthcare. The campaign defined healthcare equity as: "Providing care that does not vary in quality by personal characteristics such as ethnicity, gender, geographic location and socioeconomic status."

Last year, the campaign's focus was on raising awareness within the organization about health disparities. A toolkit provided to managers highlighted five examples:

1. Black babies are three times more likely to die in the first year of life than white babies.
2. Across the nation, American Indians/Alaska Natives have the highest death rates for diabetes and chronic lower respiratory disease of any group.
3. Blacks are referred less often than whites for cardiac catheterization and bypass grafting.
4. Latinos and blacks receive less pain medication than whites for long bone fractures in the emergency department and for cancer pain on the floors.

5. Blacks with end-stage renal disease are referred less often to the transplant list than whites.

This year the campaign has emphasized the implementation of tools to improve cross-cultural communication and competency. The third year will concentrate on integrating these principles throughout the system to make them sustainable and ensure accountability. By collecting more information from patients, the system will be positioned to determine if differences continue to exist in the preventive, diagnostic and treatment services offered to people with similar health conditions.

For more than two decades, New York's Queens Hospital Center has had an exceptionally active, assertive and influential community advisory board. The board helps ensure community health needs are identified, programs are developed and effectiveness is measured. The area's population is remarkably diverse (43 percent black, 23 percent other, 16 percent Latino, 13 percent Asian and 5 percent white), and 120 different languages are spoken by people in the service area.

Queens Hospital Center's four centers of excellence were specifically established to address the community's most significant needs: diabetes, cancer, women's health and behavioral health. Its Barbershop and Beautician Initiative is an innovative collaboration that enlists barbers and hair stylists to encourage men to receive prostate screenings and women to obtain mammograms. In addition to conducting community health fairs, the organization operates asthma and mammogram vans for those who cannot come to the hospital.

Based on data from the Office of Vital Statistics, NYC Department of Health and Mental Hygiene, the people served by Queens have had a major reduction in the years of potential life lost between 2001 and 2007, the last year for which information is available. (Years of potential life lost measures the difference between the age at death and a standard life expectancy target, typically 75 years.)

Trinity Health, based in Novi, Michigan, with 47 hospitals and a variety of other services in nine states, has approximately 47,000 employees and more than 8,000 physicians. President and CEO Joseph R. Swedish, FACHE, emphasizes that a culturally competent work force is essential to eradicating disparities and inequities in care delivery and outcomes. He believes leadership must move beyond mere rhetoric and demonstrate a moral and business commitment to a formal diversity strategy.

Trinity's strategy has seven parts: commitment and accountability, training and education, recruitment, communication, retention and development, community partners, and supplier diversity. In 2006, Trinity Health added a balanced scorecard standard titled "Circuit Breaker." At each of Trinity's sites, the CEO is required to create action plans to achieve specific diversity objectives over a period of two years. If even one of its 47 hospitals fails to meet its diversity and inclusion audit requirement, all 200 participating leaders do not receive their incentive compensation payments.

MINIMAL STEPS

A growing number of publications containing descriptions of innovative programs to reduce racial and ethnic disparities are now available. The adoption of best management practices in this area is overdue. At a minimum, two preliminary steps are a prerequisite to understanding where resources should be allocated.

1. Perform a comprehensive community health assessment on a regular basis and devote particular attention to the needs of the underserved and racial and ethnic minorities. Such an assessment is an essential component for measuring meaningful progress. With reliable baseline measures and metrics, definitive annual goals and objectives can be established and monitored.

2. Examine your organizational complexion. Equity is one of the six criteria used in evaluating applicants for the AHA-McKesson Quest for Quality Prize. For several years, the Quest for Quality Prize Committee has asked candidates to provide patient diversity demographics, specifically the percentage of Asian, black, Latino, white and other major groups. Applicants for the 2011 award are being asked to provide the same racial/ethnic background information for the governing board, medical staff, senior management, all employees and volunteers. Based on past experience, committee members have determined hospitals are more likely to demonstrate success in meeting the equity criterion when their organizational complexion mirrors that of the communities they serve.

The Agency for Healthcare Research and Quality has reported that 32 million Americans spoke a language other than English at home in 1990. By 2000, the number had risen to 52 million, which is almost 20 percent of the population. Next year, The Joint Commission will implement a new standard stipulating that hospitals effectively communicate with patients when providing care, treatment and services, and surveyors will be checking to confirm the patient's race, ethnicity and preferred language for discussing healthcare have been documented in the medical record.

Demands for increased public reporting, accountability and transparency in all spheres of our economy will not diminish. Healthcare reform will continue to be subject to intensive debate; however, successfully addressing well-documented racial and ethnic disparities should be a high priority for senior management, not because of external pressures but because we have a moral obligation to do no less.

Originally published in the September/October 2010 issue of *Healthcare Executive* magazine.

Discussion Questions

In addition to the two minimal steps recommended to determine where resources should be allocated to reduce disparities, what are some others?

Discuss how the CEOs of Trinity's 47 hospitals could increase the likelihood that each could achieve its diversity and inclusion and audit requirements.

Organizational Values Statements

William A. Nelson, PhD, HFACHE,
and Paul B. Gardent

ETHICS AND VALUES PLAY a fundamental role in healthcare organizations' culture. There are several basic characteristics of an ethically driven organization: shared mission and vision, strong inherent core values and culture, ethical practices, and ethical leadership.

Despite the importance of the organization's mission, vision and values, however, they tend to receive less leadership attention than other responsibilities such as strategy, operations and structure. The same is true regarding the attention given to creating and maintaining strong core values and ethics.

In complex healthcare organizations it is impossible to provide policies or guidelines to direct all clinical and administrative behavior or to help staff make tough decisions. As organization and management consultant and author Patrick Lencioni noted in a July 2002 *Harvard Business Review* article, "Core values are the deeply ingrained principles that guide all of a company's actions; they serve as its cultural cornerstone." An organization's core values set the standards of conduct that are considered important and therefore guide the behavior of individuals in the organization. The term "values" encompasses both right and wrong expectant behaviors.

A vision presents what the organization wants to become and gives direction for the organization's future. The mission statement delineates a clear, concise and specific description of an organization's purpose. A values statement clarifies how the organization will conduct its activities to achieve the organization's mission and vision. It is a statement about how the organization will value patients, staff, suppliers and the community. Values statements, reflecting common morality, frequently emphasize respect, integrity, trust, caring and excellence.

Where vision and mission statements describe the organization's goals, a values statement represents the core principles within the organization's culture. All staff should be aware of, accept and integrate the organization's values into their decisions and behaviors.

The organization's values can influence all the actions and decisions related to the mission and vision. For example, when a question arises regarding a trade-off between profit and quality, it is the organization's values that will likely drive the response.

Some organizational values statements are implemented effectively and serve as a guide for staff decisions and behaviors. In many organizations, however, statements are carefully crafted and adopted only to be set aside, rarely referenced or just ignored. In other organizations the values statements are treated as the latest marketing program with posters and pocket cards but little substance.

Worst of all are the organizations whose values statements conflict with the organization's actual practices and behaviors. Rather than fostering and maintaining a positive culture and setting an ethical tone for behaviors and practices, such situations undermine staff morale, breed cynicism and can lead to the acceptance of unethical practices.

NEED FOR VALUES REVIEW

The values statement should describe the guiding principles by which the staff is expected to function to achieve the organization's mission. Due to the importance of the values statement to the organization's culture, it should be regularly reviewed. This is similar to the need to periodically review clinical and administrative policy statements such as end-of-life or conflict-of-interest policies or strategic or financial plans that are regularly reviewed by executive leadership and the board.

The values review is not done primarily for the purpose of changing or modifying the wording of the values statement. Rather, the review should be an in-depth assessment of specific ethics-grounded values and the assimilation of those values into the organization's day-to-day culture, practices and behaviors of the organization's staff.

SUGGESTED VALUES REVIEW PROCESS

Following the decision to undertake an organizational values review, a values review workgroup should be established to lead the process. The workgroup should include people beyond the executive office and board. It should consist of administrative and clinical leaders; ethics, patient safety, compliance and quality improvement professionals; and community representatives. The workgroup also should consider the use of an outside resource, such as a professional who is knowledgeable in organizational ethics and cultural change, to assist with the review.

To facilitate the review, the workgroup will need to rigorously examine both the beliefs and practices within the organization. The workgroup should host a series of focus groups with frontline clinicians and staff to explore staff members' understanding of the organization's values and the extent to which the values drive their behaviors to achieve the organization's mission.

Identification of specific examples reflecting the values of the organization should be encouraged during group meetings. Those behaviors that appear to run counter to the organization's values statement also should be identified and discussed. The use of a staff survey could aid the process of understanding employees' level of awareness and application of the current values statement. In addition, the workgroup might examine how the organization's leadership actions reflect the organization's espoused values, especially when difficult decisions or conflicts arise.

This broad-based review should help determine if there is a gap between the organization's stated values and its culture and help identify areas in which there is a need for improvement. The review may also indicate a need for leadership to clarify the organization's values statement or, more likely, indicate the need for more attention to making the values a more visible and active part of the organization.

After facilitating the extensive review process, the workgroup should report to the executive leadership and board, including suggested changes to the values statement. The best values statements are not just a list of lofty words like "integrity" and "commitment"—the values statement should include a brief description for each word or phrase, providing greater detail of why and how specific values-related words or phrases are to be actualized.

An organization-wide implementation plan is essential. Without a carefully planned dissemination initiative the values statement can fail to translate into organizational practices and behaviors.

DISSEMINATION AND APPLICATION OF STATEMENTS

Leadership must own and participate in the values review process in an active and visible way. The workgroup, however, can help in the effort to disseminate the updated document throughout the organization.

The educational push of this initiative should not mean simply handing out a document but, rather, fostering discussions with leadership regarding how to make the specific values obvious and integrated throughout the organization. These discussions need not end following a formal educational thrust; discussions should be ongoing within all the organization's departments.

In addition, the values document should be a living document, regularly noted and referenced. Some of the strongest reinforcement of the organization's values comes through the stories and examples of how leadership and staff responded to difficult decisions by putting organizational values into action.

As was pointed out by Lencioni, if values are "going to really take hold in your organization, core values need to be integrated into every employee-related process—hiring methods, performance management systems, criteria for promotions and rewards, and even dismissal policies."

This review and ongoing dissemination effort will take time and commitment; in fact, it will be a continuous process. However, the time and effort are justified as they can foster the alignment of organizational values with organizational culture. Ultimately the most important way to spread organizational values is by having leadership behaviors reflect those values day in and day out.

Originally published in the March/April 2011 issue of *Healthcare Executive* magazine.

Discussion Questions

Mission and values statements serve as the core philosophy for healthcare organizations. How can leaders ensure that values statements serve as a true guide for staff decisions and behaviors?

List several examples of how a leader can serve as a role model, reflecting the organization's values.

Fear of Conflict: Management and Ethical Costs

Paul B. Hofmann, DrPH, LFACHE

FEW PEOPLE SEEK AND enjoy conflict. In fact, people generally take constructive steps to prevent and avoid it. Nonetheless, at least some conflict is inevitable, so the ability to determine which conflicts should not be averted or circumvented is a key attribute of effective executives. The other essential characteristic is the ability to manage the conflict properly.

RECOGNIZING FEAR OF CONFLICT

An old aphorism notes that one can avoid criticism by saying nothing, doing nothing and being nothing. The same might be said of conflict.

Most executives want to be liked and would prefer to say yes to requests, especially from patients and their family members, influential managers, physicians, board members and prominent citizens. Making only politically safe or popular decisions, however, is a manifestation of an executive's fear of conflict, and it is unrealistic and impractical. Competing appeals for limited resources, such as money, space and even time, make it impossible to approve every request.

Another reason executives should overcome their fear of conflict is that conflict aversion promotes a continuing tolerance for inappropriate and/or incompetent behavior. Although confronting such behavior by an employee, a physician or a board member is difficult, the costs of not taking timely action are almost always much greater.

But problems associated with making tough choices are not the only source of conflict. Conflicts also occur when subordinates in a group setting express strong differences of opinion about critical issues. An executive uncomfortable with conflict may intervene prematurely to mediate the dispute rather than allow the participants to resolve their own disagreements, potentially suppressing a productive discussion and inadvertently discouraging future candor.

Executives rarely recognize that they suffer from a fear of conflict; furthermore, subordinates and peers may not diagnose this fear and, even if they do, are unlikely to bring it to the executive's attention.

Given these factors, a candid self-appraisal is crucial. Among the warning signs that an executive is conflict averse are the following:

- Delaying key decisions beyond a reasonable time frame
- Making excessive compromises
- Rationalizing or ignoring performance problems of others, particularly if the executive hired those employees
- Withholding constructive criticism of ideas and suggestions
- Approving recommendations without a full and honest appreciation for either predictable or unintended consequences
- Smothering intense debates
- Discouraging the free expression of opposing ideas
- Delegating difficult problems, such as dealing with a disruptive physician, to a subordinate to resolve

ADDRESSING FEAR OF CONFLICT

In the July/August 2011 issue of *Healthcare Executive*, Scott Bullock, FACHE, wrote a superb CEO Focus column titled "Empowering

Staff With Communication." It discusses why successfully addressing conflict and reversing a culture of silence contribute to safer patient care. He explains how MaineGeneral Health dealt with a disturbing response to an otherwise positive employee satisfaction survey in which more than 20 percent of respondents indicated they disagreed with two statements:

- Conflict in this organization is addressed in an open manner
- People in my work group feel safe expressing their opinions/views openly

As one component of a comprehensive, systemwide approach to tackling these concerns, the MaineGeneral leadership added "speaking up" to the organization's Values and Standards, making it not only a right but "an obligation and a *moral* imperative" (italics added). Bullock describes the specific steps MaineGeneral has taken to change the organizational culture; they include implementing training based on the Crucial Conversations program by VitalSmarts, subsequently certifying a dozen senior managers to teach the program and then tracking the results.

In 1972, Ken Thomas, PhD, and Ralph Kilmann, PhD, developed the Thomas-Kilmann Conflict Mode Instrument to measure a person's behavior in conflict situations. According to an article by Thomas and Kilmann on Kilmann's website (www.kilmann.com/conflict.html), "'Conflict situations' are those in which the concerns of two people appear to be incompatible. In such situations, we can describe an individual's behavior along two basic dimensions: (1) assertiveness, the extent to which the person attempts to satisfy his (or her) own concerns, and (2) cooperativeness, the extent to which the person attempts to satisfy the other person's concerns. These two basic dimensions of behavior define five different modes for responding to conflict situations." They include competing, collaborating, compromising, accommodating and avoiding.

The article continues, "Each of us is capable of using all five conflict-handling modes. None of us can be characterized as having a single style of dealing with conflict. But certain people use some modes better than others . . . whether because of temperament or practice."

In an August 2011 article of the Center for the Health Professions at the University of California, San Francisco, Ed O'Neil, PhD, the center's director, referenced the work of Kilmann and Thomas. He wrote that six issues require consideration when trying to handle conflict in a more productive way:

1. Power—Who has the power? Is it formal or informal? How will I use my power in this conflict? Will I give up or gain power in this possible conflict?
2. Quality—Is there a 'technically correct' approach to take in this situation? Who is right in this conflict? Is it even possible to know who or what is right in this situation, or is it all opinion?
3. Importance—How important is this to me? Why? How important is it to the other party? Do I really understand why it seems important to them?
4. Time—How much time do we have to resolve this conflict? Is the clock running? Will we know more if we take more time? Is knowing more worth the effort it takes to gain that knowledge? Is my sense of time demands real or just part of my style?
5. Relationship—Is this a long-term relationship? How do I value it? Could this conflict harm the relationship? Could the way we resolve this improve the relationship?
6. Buy-in—How much engagement do I need of others to go forward? Will I lose interest if we don't account for some of my concerns?

CONCLUDING OBSERVATIONS

Conflict is a natural and normal component of a healthy work environment and should ultimately produce better decision making. But any organization that aims to achieve this balance must have a level playing field for conflict resolution and alternatives to win–lose scenarios.

The management and ethical costs of dealing poorly with conflict can be significant. Regardless of your executive position, some subordinates within your organization will probably emulate the way you handle conflict because (1) they simply assume you do so appropriately and/or (2) they believe it is an acceptable way to address conflict. Being a good role model becomes even more critical when others rely on you to demonstrate exemplary behavior by promoting candor, negotiating fairly and acting both objectively and decisively.

Healthcare employees, physicians and trustees often feel they are working in an organizational pressure cooker, experiencing more stress as a result. Conflicts can certainly add to this stress, but we must remember that an organizational culture that suppresses conflict and penalizes people who speak out is unhealthy for patients as well as staff.

Originally published in the January/February 2012 issue of *Healthcare Executive* magazine.

Discussion Questions

The author describes how an executive's fear of addressing conflicts can be detrimental to one's leadership. Briefly illustrate how such an avoidance can be detrimental to an organization.

The author suggests there are significant ethical costs for dealing poorly with conflict. Describe what those ethical costs might be.

The Importance of Failing Forward

Paul B. Hofmann, DrPH, LFACHE

According to John Maxwell, author of the 2000 book *Failing Forward*, "In life, the question is not if you will have problems, but how you are going to deal with your problems. Are you going to fail forward or backward?"

All of us will fail from time to time, but nothing counts as a mistake unless in some sense we could or should have done otherwise. Admittedly, not all mistakes are immediately identified or recognized. In many instances, the passage of time and an objective assessment of a decision's or nondecision's consequences are required.

As is frequently the case, healthcare executives can learn much from our clinical colleagues. In a fascinating study in which doctors were faced with a simulated medical emergency and had to choose from uncertain treatment options—a scenario requiring a certain amount of trial and error—doctors who paid more attention to their mistakes fared much better than those who focused on their treatment successes. The researchers concluded the better performing doctors focused more on failed treatments and gradually learned from their mistakes.

In contrast, the poorly performing doctors focused more on successful treatments, with each success confirming what the doctors (falsely) thought they knew about which treatment was better. In his article about this study appearing in the December 16, 2011, issue of

The Atlantic, Neil Wagner wrote, "Everybody makes mistakes. But far too few people take the opportunity to learn from them. We'd all be better people if we did."

FAMILIAR MISTAKES

It is difficult to imagine a healthcare executive who has not:

- Made an unwise investment decision relating to information technology or a major capital equipment purchase
- Hired or appointed the wrong person to fill a key position
- Delayed, rationalized or minimized bad news
- Tolerated the performance of an incompetent or marginally competent staff member
- Overreacted emotionally
- Devoted insufficient time to considering the potential unintended consequences of a decision
- Engaged in hyperbole to obtain approval or acceptance of a proposal
- Been less than forthright with a subordinate, a peer or an influential person—saying what you thought the individual wanted to hear rather than what you truly believed
- Responded inadequately to a crisis such as a serious preventable clinical error or the indefensible behavior of an employee or a physician
- Accepted the benefits associated with short-term gains while conceding the probability of higher long-term costs

Based on a personal experience, I add a less familiar mistake to this list: feeling so convinced by the validity and righteousness of one's position that no thought is given to the other party's alternatives and, therefore, being unprepared to propose or explore a mutually acceptable compromise. When I was the executive director of Emory University Hospital in Atlanta, the vice president for medical affairs informed me that the university president would be taking a large amount of money from the hospital's reserves to meet other university needs. The vice president said nothing could be done, but he had no objection to my meeting with the president. During the meeting, I reminded the president that our long-range financial plan, which had been approved by the university's board, depended on having the funds to support the continuing capital needs of the hospital. The president said he had no other options and asked if I felt his decision was unethical. Having great respect for this man, who was the former dean of the school of theology, I was unsure what to say and acknowledged that he was in a difficult position.

Because I was so convinced of the validity of my position, neglected to consider the president's position and had failed to think in advance of possible alternatives, it was not until the next day that I sent him a recommendation proposing he borrow rather than take funds from the hospital's reserves. Still vividly remembering my initial mistake and my appropriate but belated effort to correct it, I hope this painful encounter has permitted me to fail forward when faced with subsequent situations and comparable feelings of self-righteousness.

CREATING AN ENVIRONMENT FOR FAILING FORWARD

When considering the list of familiar mistakes, we know many of them may have been due to insufficient or inaccurate information, lack of expert input, time constraints, ignorance of legitimate alternatives, carelessness, political pressure, a conflict of interest, undue haste or a failure to follow established policies and/or external requirements. However, if avoiding mistakes simply meant recognizing and avoiding these problems, then the solutions seem fairly self-evident.

The key to improving management performance is not just minimizing mistakes but learning from the ones we inevitably make. To accurately assess the prospects for failing forward, we must ask:

- How is making a mistake viewed in our organization?
- Is a fear of anger, embarrassment or retribution inhibiting staff from making decisions, taking initiative or accepting reasonable risks?
- Within reasonable limits, is the freedom to fail empty rhetoric or genuine?
- Who can be trusted to counsel us and provide a candid appraisal of possible options in a time of crisis?
- What steps should be considered to maximize failing forward individually and institutionally?

The ability to answer these and similar questions is fundamental to creating an organizational environment where staff members are both permitted and encouraged to fail forward. We should begin by recognizing mistakes, rectifying them where possible and using them as positive learning opportunities, creating and maintaining a climate where failure is not viewed as a career-limiting event. If an organizational culture supports only those managers who are totally risk averse, it is much less likely to attract or retain leaders who are innovative and creative.

Acting on the courage of one's convictions, particularly under stressful conditions, involves an element of professional risk, but highly capable people should be prepared to accept both the risk and the possible perception of failure when circumstances compel them to act courageously.

CONCLUDING OBSERVATIONS

Compared to clinicians, executives are less likely to critique their mistakes either formally or informally, so evidence-based management practices are not well documented, disseminated, promoted or adopted. In the absence of the information that results from evidence-based management, we substantially reduce our opportunities to fail forward. Ethically, we do a disservice to our patients, staff, organizations and communities by neglecting to capitalize on our collective experiences and insights.

But in many respects, believing that our failures are largely due to the unwillingness or reluctance of others to share best practices is a convenient excuse. If we don't accept accountability for mistakes, our progress will certainly be impeded. Maxwell suggests people who fail backward blame others, repeat the same mistakes and expect never to fail again. In contrast, he describes people who fail forward as those who take responsibility, learn from each mistake and know failure is a part of progress.

Most successful people admit they learned more from their mistakes than from their successes. I suggest that failure is not avoidable, but not learning from our failures is. Finally, given our fallibility, we should be diligent in forgiving others who have learned from their mistakes as well as forgiving ourselves.

Originally published in the May/June 2012 issue of *Healthcare Executive* magazine.

Discussion Questions

An argument is being made that all executives will make mistakes but need to learn from those mistakes. How can the failure to learn from one's mistakes undermine the ethical foundation of the organization?

What can an executive do to ensure that the concept of learning from mistakes is built into the organization's culture?

Moral Management as a Leadership Priority

Frankie Perry, RN, LFACHE

In the June 6, 2013, cover story in *Bloomberg Businessweek*, "The Cheapest, Happiest Company in the World: Costco, where toilet paper—and ecstatic employees—can both be found in bulk," Costco CEO Craig Jelinek attributes much of the company's financial and market success to treating its employees well. In a 2013 letter to Congress addressing raising the federal minimum wage Jelinek wrote: "We know it's a lot more profitable in the long term to minimize employee turnover and maximize employee productivity, commitment and loyalty."

Putting employees first must be working because all indicators show Costco outpacing its competitors. The Costco experience about the value in treating employees well and managing them in an ethically responsible way draws considerable parallels to healthcare.

In its *Code of Ethics*, ACHE provides clear guidelines for healthcare executives' ethical and professional obligations to employees. Most center on creating and contributing to a work environment and culture that promotes and supports ethical conduct within the organization. Organizational culture, ethical standards and a safe and healthy work environment are essential in fulfilling one's ethical responsibilities to employees.

But while the "right" policies and procedures and the "right" culture and work environment may be in place to promote the ethical treatment of employees, it is the day-to-day management actions that determine whether managers are fulfilling their ethical responsibilities to the employees they supervise.

MAINTAINING AN ETHICAL CULTURE

Creating an infrastructure that includes such things as a code of ethics, standards of conduct and an ethics committee may be the easy management task; making ethical conduct the norm throughout the organization from the boardroom to housekeeping is a much more difficult task.

More than anything, managers who role model ethical conduct in the treatment of their employees send a clear message about what is acceptable behavior in the organization. Employees who are treated with honesty, fairness and respect are more likely in turn to treat patients, clients, vendors and co-workers in this same way, thus contributing to the success of the organization in its many business and professional relationships inherent in healthcare delivery.

RECRUITMENT AND HIRING PRACTICES

Competent, ethical clinical and nonclinical employees want to work for an ethical organization with leaders who inspire and challenge them to achieve high levels of ethical performance. A culture where staff and employees are treated ethically and are expected to treat others in a like manner will attract and retain a workforce that will enhance the image of the institution.

When recruiting staff, it is sometimes tempting to oversell your organization and its position in the marketplace. This is understandable in your desire to attract highly qualified people. But it is not fair to the recruit to paint an unrealistic picture of the organization and its viability or of the position, its authority and responsibilities, especially if the recruit will be relocating his or her family and committing considerable investment in relocation.

When making a job offer to a new hire, it is a questionable practice to offer more compensation to a new hire than what an existing employee who has tenure and experience in your organization and who is doing a good job at the same level with the same responsibilities is receiving. Caution must be exercised to ensure equitable compensation, benefits and support for staff members.

In addition, hiring or promoting a staff person into a position, giving him or her clear expectations of the job to be done and then failing to provide the resources or the authority needed for the employee to meet those required expectations is unfair to both the employee and the organization.

MANAGING DIVERSITY

Failure to understand the importance of having a cross-cultural workforce will increasingly thwart the achievement of organizational goals and set the stage for discrimination of employees based on factors such as race, ethnicity, national origin, gender, religion, age, marital status, sexual orientation, gender identity or disability. To avoid derailment of organizational goals and the threat of potential litigation, healthcare leaders must create, embrace and sustain a culture of diversity that serves the needs of the workforce and patients.

A recent legal action charging a hospital with employee discrimination based on race made national news. A parent demanded that nursing staff of a different race than himself not be assigned to care for his child. The parent's demand was met in spite of a hospital policy to the contrary. This case points out the need for staff education, especially of front-line workers, related to anti-discrimination laws and policies and their application to the workforce.

Much has been written in academic literature and in the media about sexual harassment, and yet these cases continue to make news. In an ethical organization, management will establish a zero tolerance policy for sexual harassment, make certain employees are well educated in the law, and assign designated staff members to investigate and handle complaints and answer questions other employees may have.

PERFORMANCE EVALUATIONS

In an ethical organization, performance evaluations will be fair, honest, objective, timely and focused on the work. Consistent standards of performance will be applied to all staff. Employees will not be expected to perform beyond their job descriptions or beyond what can reasonably be expected of them given the resources they have been provided. Managers will not imply that poor performance may be the result of such factors as aging, health or family issues that may be viewed as discriminatory and open the organization up to litigation or disability claims.

Managers often view performance evaluations as a bureaucratic necessity—not a high priority on their to-do list. They may even allow considerable time to lapse beyond the due date for the review. This can be especially unfair to the employee if a pay raise is contingent upon the completion of a satisfactory performance evaluation. Even if this is not the case, employees deserve to know if they are doing a good job, if there are areas of their job performance that require improvement and how improvements might be facilitated and measured.

COMMUNICATION

Ethical managers practice two-way communication with their workforce. They seek employees' opinions and ideas, encourage civil debate and avoid the practice of listening only to those who agree with their position.

Ethical managers recognize that any threat to the status quo or existing stability of the organization such as workforce reduction, mergers or acquisitions will have a direct impact on the job security of individual employees. Employees need sufficient information to mobilize personal resources to plan or take action if needed. It is unfair to withhold information from employees that may allow them to make necessary adjustments for themselves or their families.

Managers must not lose sight of the fact that employees' job satisfaction, loyalty, commitment and productivity are in large part directly related to how they are treated by their "boss"—not primarily by the organization or human resources department—but by their manager. It is the day-to-day decisions imbedded in routine management functions that reflect the moral treatment of the workforce, which in turn reflects the character of the leadership and, in turn, the character and image of the organization.

Originally published in the January/February 2014 issue of *Healthcare Executive* magazine.

Discussion Questions

Briefly describe the organizational barriers or challenges to being a morally driven leader.

The author suggests that performance evaluations can be a tool for fostering moral management. Describe how an organization's mission and values might be used in performance evaluations.

The Ethics of Hospital Security

John J. Donnellan Jr., FACHE

WORKPLACE VIOLENCE IN HOSPITALS and healthcare settings is a serious and frequent occurrence. According to a March 2011 report by the U.S. Department of Justice, approximately 10 percent of victims of nonfatal workplace violence (rape/sexual assault, robbery, and aggravated and simple assault occurring while at work or on duty) are employed in medical occupations. And, among the occupations measured, the rate of violence experienced by healthcare workers was exceeded only by law enforcement personnel and persons employed in retail sales, especially bartenders and gas station attendants.

A recent survey by Karen Gabel Speroni, PhD, RN, and colleagues of nurses employed in urban/community hospital systems in the mid-Atlantic region of the United States—as reported in the September 2013 issue of the *Journal of Emergency Nursing*—found that 76 percent of survey respondents reported experiencing verbal or physical abuse in the past year by patients or visitors. Clearly, security and violence prevention is a matter requiring the attention of healthcare executives and board members.

Healthcare organizations pose a unique security challenge. These institutions must be accessible, frequently 24 hours a day. Patients may be unresponsive upon arrival or may experience periods of temporary or permanently limited capacity throughout their stay. Methods traditionally employed to prevent on-site violence or deter the introduction of weapons (identification and background checks, searches of persons or property, etc.) are often limited by the organization's need to provide rapid care, especially emergency care.

Furthermore, the condition for which an individual seeks treatment (e.g., substance abuse, trauma associated with criminal behavior) may be unavoidably coupled with the individual's potential for violence. Given these dynamics, what should healthcare executives do to meet their ethical obligation to provide patients and staff alike with a safe, violence-free environment? Let's begin by examining the expectations of key stakeholders: patients, communities, staff members and organizational leaders.

STAKEHOLDER EXPECTATIONS

Communities and patients expect that healthcare organizations will provide care that is effective and of quality consistent with generally accepted standards of practice. They expect care to be accessible when needed and provided without prejudice.

Patients expect that family members, domestic partners and close friends are free to visit and provide them physical, emotional and spiritual comfort, and participate in important decisions about their care. They expect information about their illness and treatment will be kept private and shared only with those whom they designate or who need to know. They expect to be free from harm, including willful harm, by those providing care and accidental or unintended harm caused by error. And they expect their care will be provided in a nonviolent environment.

Hospital employees generally recognize that there are risks inherent to working in a healthcare institution, but they do not expect to be exposed to unnecessary danger. They expect organizational leaders will take necessary and reasonable steps to keep them, and the patients they care for, free from accidental harm (through programs to monitor and reduce workplace hazard and injury), and free from violence and abuse brought about by patients, visitors and other staff members.

Healthcare leaders have an ethical responsibility to meet community, patient and employee expectations regarding quality, access, privacy and safety. However, they must exercise this responsibility in a manner aligned with the organization's mission and values.

EXAMINING CONFLICTS

Unfortunately, meeting one set of expectations often creates conflict with another, posing an ethical dilemma for the healthcare executive. Consider the conflicts created in the following scenarios:

> ***Case 1:*** An HIV-positive patient with a history of violent behavior and noncompliance with prescribed psychotropic medication is undergoing chronic dialysis. In a recent episode, the patient became agitated and removed and threw IV lines, causing a nurse to be stuck with a contaminated needle. As a result of this incident a number of resident physicians and nurses have refused to care for this patient and demand that the patient be denied further treatment at the hospital. Other providers disagree, stating that the institution and staff have a moral obligation to continue to care for this patient.
>
> ***Case 2:*** A recent series of verbal and physical assaults on ED staff occurred while they were conducting triage examinations of patients demonstrating symptoms of psychiatric illness. As a result, ED staff and labor representatives demand that psychiatric examinations in the ED be conducted on these patients in the presence of a hospital police officer or in an examination room furnished with audio and visual observation equipment and monitored by police located nearby and able to respond immediately in the event of a crisis. Many other

staff members, including patient advocates, object, noting that such actions are prejudicial to persons with mental illness, a violation of a patient's right to privacy and a violation of the confidentiality of the provider–patient relationship.

Case 3: Hospital executives, concerned about a rise in workplace violence in their community and the particular risks faced by hospitals, plan to install imaging technology at the hospital entrance to scan all staff, patients and visitors, along with their personal property, upon entering the building. In addition, they plan to install hidden surveillance cameras at various undisclosed locations throughout the institution to allow hospital police to monitor activity in areas determined to be at risk for violent behavior. Hospital leaders, security experts and many staff members believe this to be a prudent strategy that is in the best interests of employees and patients. However, many other staff members object, believing it is an unwelcome and unnecessary invasion of the privacy and confidentiality of both patients and employees.

RESOLVING CONFLICT

The cases above describe situations in which multiple expectations of various stakeholders, each of which the healthcare executive has an ethical responsibility to uphold, are in conflict. Resolution requires the following:

- The recognition by stakeholders (staff members, patients and communities) that the nature of services provided by hospitals involves risk, and mitigating risk may require security measures more intrusive than one might expect in their home or in places of commerce with less inherent risk.

- The recognition by leaders that security measures, however necessary, must be respectful of employee, patient, community and organizational values, and be as transparent as possible. Security management must be approached as not simply a matter of crime prevention and law enforcement, but as an ethical responsibility. This requires that security and law enforcement practices be established and carried out with an appreciation of organizational values and divergent but legitimate points of view about the nature and the extent of security measures put into effect.
- A commitment to ongoing education and open communication about security measures planned and in place, and what staff, patients and visitors alike can do to improve safety and security at the institution.
- These objectives can only be achieved through partnership with all stakeholders. Healthcare executives should initiate a clear and deliberative process by which security policies and measures are offered, established, implemented and regularly reexamined to ensure consistency with the organization's mission and ethical values. The process should be guided by executives, trustees and the organization's ethics committee, and include patients, community leaders, employees and labor officials. And the process must be ongoing.

It is important to recognize that regardless of the processes established, conflicts will occur. The organization's ethics committee should be available to mediate future conflicts and make recommendations to prevent conflict re-occurrence.

Originally published in the May/June 2014 issue of *Healthcare Executive* magazine.

Discussion Questions

The author describes the moral imperative to safeguard staff in an environment of increased violence in the workplace. Are there situations when staff members are morally justified to discharge a violent patient?

Describe the role of the healthcare executive in ensuring the safety of staff.

Ensuring Patient-Centered Care

William A. Nelson, PhD, HFACHE,
and Thom Walsh, PhD

THERE ARE SOME HEALTHCARE needs that can be easily identified and accepted by patients. The patient with a hip fracture is readily diagnosed and, according to evidence-based care, requires hospitalization. However, easily diagnosed conditions with well-accepted, evidence-based care pathways are unusual. More commonly, healthcare involves less certainty, and the "best" course of treatment often involves choosing between two or more beneficial options. Such situations beg for true patient-centered care.

Aligning a healthcare delivery system with patients' informed preferences is the goal and promise of patient-centered care. In 2001, the Institute of Medicine's report, "Crossing the Quality Chasm: A New Healthcare System for the 21st Century," described patient-centered care as one of six interrelated aims that are essential for delivering high-quality healthcare. According to the IOM, the patient-centered aim is to provide "care that is respectful of and responsive to individual patient preferences, needs, and values, and ensuring that patient values guide all clinical decisions." Patient-centered care has been the battle cry for hospitals ever since.

Since the IOM first introduced the patient-centered aim, a torrent of wide-ranging activities have occurred under this banner, ranging from fresh coats of paint, to improved signage that helps guide patients' movement within a hospital, to emphasizing compassionate care and transparency. Despite being important initiatives, these activities failed to fully grasp the ethical component of patient-centered care. Patient-centered care is achieved by consistently eliciting informed patient preferences and ensuring those preferences are integrated into the care plan.

How are patients' preferences consistently elicited and integrated and what role do organizational leaders have in ensuring these processes occur? Despite the diverse areas of attention given to patient-centered care, the central focus needs to be on fostering enhanced patient–provider communication and collaborative decision making. Shared decision making is at the core of patient-centered care. It requires providers to invite patients to actively engage in robust communication in which clinicians provide information regarding the risks and benefits of treatment choices, make an effort to elicit patients' preferences and integrate the informed patient's preferences into an individualized care plan.

Because shared decision making is so central to the true meaning of patient-centered care and organizational values, leaders need to ensure processes for eliciting informed patients' choices are the norm rather than an exception. Healthcare policy makers, regulatory bodies and some healthcare executives are developing approaches to ensure that it is a consistently applied practice in delivery of all care.

HEALTHCARE LEADERS' ROLE

The Affordable Care Act has raised the profile of shared decision making still further but has also generated confusion about what it means to implement shared decision making. Without clarity about the concept and required training and skills, it is easy to confuse shared decision-making skills with patient decision support tools (e.g., educational videos, option grids, websites and leaflets). These tools augment a skilled provider's shared decision making, and they can be helpful for sharing information with patients, but they do not ensure patient-centered communication between patient and provider or integration of preferences into the care plan.

We propose healthcare leaders have an integral role to play to ensure patient-centered care is meaningful. To achieve the IOM aim of enhancing patient–provider decision making, there needs to be an organization-wide focus on ensuring that the concept moves beyond just a tagline in a value statement to consistent application in all provider–patient engagements.

In the February 2014 issue of the *Journal of General Internal Medicine*, Michael L. Millenson notes that "Behaviors formerly presented as ideals are being reframed to include benchmarks such as one might see in a financial plan." Behaviors once described as ideals by the IOM need to be reframed as organizational benchmarks. In other words, the fulfillment of the patient-centered aim cannot be left to chance. Leaders must prioritize it and measure it.

Measurement data is the key to Millenson's description of an "ongoing change from aspirational goals to operational ones in patient-centeredness." With this shift from a broad ideal to a more regulated approach to patient-centered care, organizational leaders must ensure that provider–patient decision making consistently reflects a shared decision-making process. For organizations to fully move in such a direction requires the organization's leadership to ensure that patient-centered care is the normative behavior of healthcare providers. To embrace the concept of patient-centered care, organizational leadership will need to:

Understand the scope and value of patient-centered care. Leaders need to demonstrate a full understanding and support of the patient-centered care concept and its ethical value.

Ensure providers embrace and implement patient-centered care. Leaders must collaborate to ensure frontline healthcare providers understand, accept and implement shared decision-making skills. Training is crucial if providers are to learn the skills. And executives must support training. For example, a concerted effort is required to measure the effectiveness of the communication process between providers and patients. It is not enough to simply count the number of decision support tools disseminated.

Address barriers preventing patient-centered care. Leaders need to acknowledge and reconcile organizational barriers in the implementation of patient-centered care, including the current reimbursement models that often limit the clinician's time for necessary, expanded patient engagement.

Ensure patient information and tools are available. The availability and use of patient decision support tools are part of patient-centered care, but the tools do not replace communication skills. Decision support tools need to be regularly assessed and evaluated for their ability to assist providers' and patients' efforts to integrate informed patient preferences into individualized care plans.

Monitor the quality of patient–provider decision making. Leaders, in collaboration with providers, must implement routine processes that measure patient-centered care. The CollaboRATE project at The Dartmouth Center for Health Care Delivery Science and The Dartmouth Institute for Health Policy & Clinical Practice at Dartmouth College, Hanover, New Hampshire, developed a survey that can provide clinicians and administrators with data regarding patient-centered care (www.collaboratescore.org). The survey asks patients three questions using a 1–9 scale: "How much effort was made to help you understand your health issues? How much effort was made to listen to the things that matter most to you about your health issues? And, how much effort was made to include what matters most to you in choosing what to do next?"

Measured at the clinic level, this feedback helps executives know which delivery units are "walking the talk." The survey provides a wealth of information for providers and executives. For example, it provides insights into whether additional provider training is needed or if clinicians are fulfilling best practice protocols.

Assess the effectiveness of patient-centered care. Assessment results should be collated and shared. This process is not conducted to cast blame, but, rather, to determine where further training efforts are needed, where system issues need to be altered, where barriers need to be addressed or where care processes need to be redesigned to further patient-centered care. When effective patient-centered care is achieved, it can be celebrated and marketed to the community.

Patient-centered care is more than a banner on a website; it is a fundamental change from a traditional provider decision-making process to a patient engagement approach that fosters reciprocal sharing of information, preference solicitation and integration in care. Aligning the care patients receive with their informed preferences is the essence of patient-centered care. Training is needed for providers to learn needed skills, and measurement is also needed to monitor the implementation of true patient-centered care. Healthcare executives must play an active role in leading and celebrating the change.

Originally published in the July/August 2014 issue of *Healthcare Executive* magazine.

Discussion Questions

Patient-centered care has been called a rallying cry for all organizations. If you, as the organization's leader, were charged with developing a patient-centered plan, what would you include in your plan?

The authors described the importance of leaders taking an active role in guiding a patient-centered organization. What specific metrics could be used to assess whether patient-centered care exists throughout the organization?

Avoiding Blinded Healthcare Leadership

William A. Nelson, PhD, HFACHE

In the book *Managerial Ethics in Healthcare* (Health Administration Press, 2014), the authors drive home the point that "the single most important responsibility of a healthcare administrator is to ensure the moral core of his healthcare organization remains intact as the organization faces increasing challenges to its operations and even its viability." Addressing such challenges requires leaders to first be aware of the ethical challenges or concerns that arise in the healthcare delivery of their organizations.

In 2009, Atul Gawande, MD, authored an article in *The New Yorker* titled "The Cost Conundrum," which speaks directly about healthcare spending but also healthcare leadership. The article is often referenced and used as an assigned reading in healthcare management courses. It explores healthcare spending in two cities about 800 miles apart. The two communities are described as being similar demographically (population, public health statistics, number of immigrants, unemployment, etc.). Yet, Gawande notes, that using the best approximation of overall healthcare spending—Medicare expenditures—spending in one city is twice what it is in the other city.

As Gawande explored the reasons for such diverse spending patterns he met with a group of physicians from the higher-spending city. After telling the physicians healthcare spending in their city was among the highest in the United States, they offered several responses. The physicians were initially dubious about the data, but then they began offering justifications for the spending differences, including better service and malpractice costs. Following some discussion regarding those possibilities a surgeon finally got to the heart of the matter and said, "Come on . . . there is overutilization here," suggesting racking up charges with extra tests, services and procedures as the culprit.

Later, Gawande met with healthcare executives to explore the spending differences between the two cities. When he shared the same spending information he had shared with the physicians, one healthcare executive's response was surprise that spending was so high but that, while it was interesting, she could not explain the reasoning behind the high costs. The executive offered some potential explanations, but then continued to be puzzled. Another executive, when informed of the extent of spending, offered what Gawande described as reflective explanations for utilization patterns. It is clear, however, the executives were unaware of what the Medicare data was indicating regarding the big picture of healthcare spending.

Such a realization suggests an important problem in the science of healthcare delivery: Do healthcare executives have a clear and accurate picture of what is going on in their own organizations? Or are they blind to what is really occurring within the organization related to unrecognized ethical concerns?

WHAT IS A BLINDED LEADER?

The authors of *Managerial Ethics in Healthcare* define a blinded leader as one who "does not recognize or understand the moral complexities or consequences before her." Consequently, a blinded leader is incapable of fulfilling his or her ethical responsibility to maintain the organization's moral foundation. Due to a lack of understanding of what is actually occurring, healthcare executives can miss the obvious—that the organization's practices and culture are out of line with the organization's stated values.

There appear to be two fundamental forms of leadership blindness. The first is the situation in which the executive has either flawed or incomplete information. Thus, the lack of adequate information can create blind spots in recognizing the presence of ethical challenges within one's organization. The result of such blindness can affect decision making or, in some situations, result in lack of needed action.

The second form of blindness is based on what cognitive scientists describe as mental images that actually can be misperceptions. Healthcare professionals possess deeply held assumptions or beliefs that can frame how they understand or perceive their organizations. Those sets of generalizations can significantly influence not only how the leader views the organization but can also influence the leader's behaviors and decisions, including one's moral actions. These ingrained mental perceptions become the lenses through which an individual views the organization.

Such mental images can be a powerful force that shapes how the organization is experienced. Deeply held assumptions can influence a leader's perception or viewpoint about the need for organizational change. For example, the hospital administrator may believe the organization is living its value statement in both clinical and administrative practices or is serving the healthcare needs of the community even though an objective, accurate read of the environment would show otherwise.

Maybe that is why the administrators in the Gawande article repeatedly stated, "That's interesting," when hearing about the spending pattern. Performing unnecessary tests and procedures that provide no benefit implies staff members are neither acting in the best interest of patients nor providing full disclosure of the interventions in a shared decision-making process. The healthcare leader may inadvertently be blinded because his or her mental image is, "Of course we only act in the patient's best interest."

Removing blinders requires healthcare leaders to recognize that all executives possess a certain level of cognitive images of themselves and the organization around them. And those images, similar to incomplete data, may be false or at least not fully accurate in capturing the reality of the organization. As Paul Batalden, MD, Dartmouth professor and founding chair of the Institute for Healthcare Improvement, has stated, unfortunately some professionals have a well-developed capacity to rationalize away the newsworthiness of potentially disconfirming data and assessments that clearly point to the need to improve quality, value and the ethical integrity of the organization.

For the executives in the Gawande article, having accurate information could break down limited insight and lead to change that reflects the organization's values. Therefore, healthcare leaders need accurate lenses through which to understand the organization's actual practices. To foster greater clarity in understanding what is occurring within the organization that may need to change, executives may consider the following approaches as well as others developed at their organization.

COLLECTING RELEVANT DATA

Healthcare executives should review locally developed data focusing on primary clinical indicators of quality and be aware of data that compares their facility to other healthcare organizations and national standards. For example, the Dartmouth Atlas (www.dartmouthatlas.org) has documented glaring variations in how medical resources are used in the United States. The project uses Medicare data to provide comprehensive information and analysis about national, regional and local markets, as well as individual hospitals and their affiliated physicians.

TRUTHFUL FEEDBACK

Healthcare executives need to have an accurate picture of their organization's patient care delivery practices. In addition to data, a great source of insight is an organization's staff members. They must be able to openly express issues or concerns when they perceive the organization's values as not synergistic with actual practices. Such expressions should be encouraged rather than discouraged or written off as merely complaints of a disgruntled employee.

Expressions of concerns or problems should be encouraged in an environment free from retribution. Such an expectation needs to be the normative management practice. As professionals, we do not always like to hear about concerns or problems, but listening to them can lead to an enhanced understanding of organizational practices, including those suggesting a need for change. Promoting straight talk from staff can lead to a better culture and an organization linked to its values.

LEADERSHIP ENGAGEMENT

Another approach to improved organizational clarity is getting out of the administrative offices and meeting rooms to visit staff and patients in all areas of the facility. Yes, that may be logistically challenging, so various members of the executive team may have to visit different areas of the facility. The point is to foster engagement, interaction and two-way communication with front-line staff.

The challenging demands on healthcare executives require having accurate information and insight. Lack of clear, accurate information can create a false understanding that all is fine.

Additionally, leaders' mental images of their organizations can be far from reality—the mental lenses through which a professional understands the organization's present practices may be less than accurate. If executives cannot step out of their mental image they will be unable to recognize where actual behaviors diverge from stated values. Healthcare leaders need to develop approaches to ensure the accuracy of their images so that daily clinical and administrative practices are clearly aligned with the organization's values.

Originally published in the November/December 2014 issue of *Healthcare Executive* magazine.

Discussion Questions

The author illustrates how blind leadership can give an inaccurate understanding of the organization. Briefly describe how such a misunderstanding can impact the alignment of the organization's values with staff behaviors.

To avoid blind leadership, describe assessment tools that can provide leaders with a clear understanding of whether the organization is aligned to its mission and values.

CEO Ethical Considerations in Right-Sizing

Frankie Perry, RN, LFACHE

HEALTHCARE LEADERS AND THOSE aspiring to be leaders must recognize first and foremost that character and integrity constitute the very cornerstone of leadership. Organizations have failed and promising careers have been derailed when ethics have been relegated to secondary importance or, worse yet, ignored in the pursuit of more bottom-line considerations.

In this article, an excerpt from the book *The Tracks We Leave: Ethics & Management Dilemmas in Healthcare*, second edition (Health Administration Press, 2013), we explore the real ethical considerations regarding workforce reduction (particularly nurse staffing) at the fictional Hillside County Medical Center located in an urban Midwest setting.

The difficulties in recruiting nurses and the financial requirements of tight staffing have increased the need for overtime and mandatory overtime. Not only does it mean higher costs, but concerns about the strain on staff and the effect of excessive overtime on the clinical care quality also have prompted state legislatures to develop controls regarding the use of overtime. Increased overtime also stimulates reaction from unions, which can result in strikes and other work actions.

These combined pressures have resulted in the difficulties that Hillside currently faces. The CEO and management staff have examined their situation and realized that unless significant changes are made quickly, Hillside's financial viability will be compromised. The CEO also recognizes that these issues are more important today than previously. His board, like many, has increasingly identified the hospital's operating margin and financial performance as the primary indicator of the management team's effectiveness. In addition, the size and complexity of today's healthcare capital expenses result in an increasing dependence on the bond market, which puts great significance on bond ratings from recognized financial assessment organizations.

Many questions are sure to arise given this scenario: What is the most appropriate and ethical method of addressing the organization's potential financial shortcomings? To whom should the CEO listen as he determines the appropriate course of action? Should he include others beyond senior management? If so, whom? How does the CEO prioritize financial viability as compared with clinical quality, organizational mission and community responsibilities? Is right-sizing the only answer or even the best answer to addressing financial difficulties? Does right-sizing ensure that all levels and groups in the organization share the effect of and exposure to these difficulties? Can right-sizing successfully address financial deficiencies without compromising clinical needs? Should the CEO examine other options to address the organization's financial concerns? Does the approach ensure that the effect of the decision does not create even bigger difficulties in the long run?

In addition to these important questions, a main consideration when right-sizing is that patient care must not be compromised in any cost-saving effort. With that said, the CEO must consider four important elements in a workforce reduction pertaining to nurses: medical staff, governing board, unions and hospitals, and health system employees.

MEDICAL STAFF

The medical staff have evolved as an informal (and sometimes formal) representative for hospital staff; they likely will hear all the rumors (accurate or not), know the staff's fears, and, in many cases, attempt to defend and protect the staff. Such attempts may include discussions with board members or use of the formal medical staff structure to react to any considered changes or reductions. Because right-sizing is difficult to do without affecting services, in some circumstances their concerns may be legitimate. More important, the medical staff can be valuable when determining how to address this problem. The CEO must understand that the medical staff will be affected and should be a part of the process in some way. They can be defensive and disruptive, or they can be collaborative. Because financial problems are unfortunately common in healthcare, members of the medical staff no longer think of staff reductions as inconceivable. Accordingly, the CEO may identify this challenge as one that requires the combined efforts of both the medical staff and management. The CEO should start by educating and sharing his concerns with the medical staff in a variety of settings. Using the formal structure, beginning with the medical executive committee, is beneficial.

However, informal discussions at departmental meetings or with key individual physicians also are essential. The medical staff can contribute greatly to the resolution of this problem. Reductions in length of stay, selection and use of medical and surgical supplies, and increases in admissions are possible and may be preferable alternatives to losing popular staff or important services.

Finally, involvement in these tough decisions may enhance the medical staff's appreciation that, after thorough analysis, the chosen approach is the most feasible one.

GOVERNING BOARD MEMBERS

The board will be involved in the formal approval stages of the process, but they may provide value in the decision phase as well. Because rightsizing is increasingly common in other industries, some board members may have experience in this area. The CEO must be willing to use all available expertise to accomplish staff reductions with the least negative effect. The more involved the board is, the more support this matter will receive and the better prepared board members will be when responding to any personal inquiries they may receive regarding actions taken.

UNIONS

The increasing involvement of unions has required senior managers to develop new skills to work successfully in a union environment. Although the most common approach U.S. managers take when planning right-sizing is to notify unions of the plan for reductions, the CEO should strongly consider involving union leadership at an earlier stage of the process. Sharing the problem and identifying it as an issue common to all parties may direct negative feelings away from the hospital and management and focus attention on the external forces that are causing the financial problems. In addition, union leadership may have valuable input.

Just as important, involving union leadership in solving the problem demonstrated the difficulty that management was facing and its desire to reduce costs in the best and fairest manner possible. Essential to the success of this approach with union leadership and employees are the following actions:

- The first cuts must be made at the level of vice president, associate administrator or senior departmental director.
- No particular department or segment of the organization should be exempt from right-sizing, unless this exemption is completely justifiable.
- If possible, the same percentage of managers as of employees should be dismissed.
- Managers should exhibit and communicate to their employees the sacrifices they are making as a result of the right-sizing.

These actions will allow union leaders to return to their respective constituents with a strong appreciation of the challenge involved and the intent of management to address rightsizing fairly.

EMPLOYEES

Communication with employees is critical as the issue develops. Rumors, misinformation and anger toward management are not beneficial and are traditionally disruptive and counterproductive. It is an ethical responsibility to employees that you communicate with them early on. It is unfair and unethical to spring information on employees without adequate time to prepare for their transition.

The CEO is responsible for defining guidelines that ensure all staff resources are incorporated into the process, even over the recommendations of management who prefer to make these decisions the easy way. Fear of politically affecting the process and of delaying needed reductions is common, and while such caution has merit, this is not the time for management to be autocratic. When properly managed, right-sizing can lay the foundation for a new, vibrant organization.

The primary goal in rightsizing is to improve overall financial viability. The organization is measured on its financial viability, which is essential to its long-term success. The CEO should remember that if cutting costs was the only goal, then closing all the nursing units would do the trick—a large percentage of costs would be eliminated; however, the corresponding loss of revenue obviously precludes that approach.

To quote from noted ethicist Paul B. Hofmann, DrPH, "A wise and experienced healthcare executive whom I know once observed that 'working in healthcare gives you the opportunity to do something ethical every day.'"

Originally published in the May/June 2016 issue of *Healthcare Executive* magazine.

Discussion Questions

The author summarizes four vital elements when developing a workforce reduction plan. How would you prioritize them and why?

Increasingly, hospitals facing financial difficulties are exploring mergers and acquisition options. When should this possibility be explored and what prerequisites should be considered to ensure an ethics-grounded culture?

Exposing the Shadows of Compromise

Paul B. Hofmann, DrPH, LFACHE

Competent healthcare professionals can and do disagree with one another about critical issues. Usually motivated by their strong convictions and genuine passion, they will offer compelling arguments to convince those who take opposing views to see things their way. However, the need for compromise must be considered when unanimity cannot be achieved.

ALL COMPROMISES ARE NOT SIMILARLY MOTIVATED

Martin Benjamin, author of *Splitting the Difference: Compromise and Integrity in Ethics and Politics*, suggests there are three types of compromise, two of which are ethically acceptable and one that is not: compromise as outcome and process, compromise as prudence and compromise as betrayal.

Most often, people are engaged in the first type of compromise, which may involve a difference in views about what to do in a particular situation or how to accomplish the desired outcome. Discussion of respective advantages and disadvantages of each position occurs, and relatively quickly, an accommodation is reached that is acceptable to both parties.

Compromise as prudence usually involves a more detailed examination of external factors, constraints and conditions. The time to achieve a mutually agreeable solution may take longer, but the participants eventually agree on the best course of action for the individuals involved and their organization.

The first two types of compromise share two basic elements. Although they both involve concessions to reach common ground and a solution that is mutually beneficial, there is no shift in fundamental personal values or beliefs. In contrast, compromise as betrayal suggests the negotiator has ceded values and principles and equivocated to the extent that his or her credibility and integrity are placed at risk.

THE HIGH COST OF COMPROMISED INTEGRITY

In their essay "Moral Residue"—published in *Margin of Error: The Ethics of Mistakes in the Practice of Medicine*—George C. Webster and Francoise E. Baylis make a significant observation. They state eloquently, "The experience of compromised integrity that involves the setting aside or violation of deeply held (and publicly professed) beliefs, values and principles can sear the heart." If the person succumbs to organizational pressures and ultimately suppresses long-held beliefs, values and principles, he or she turns into what Webster and Baylis have described as a "moral chameleon," thereby becoming "desensitized to wrongdoing, willing to tolerate morally questionable or morally impermissible actions."

So what is the message for healthcare professionals? It is easy to espouse and demonstrate ethical behavior when convenient, but much harder to do so when your manager, department head, vice president, CEO or board chair has a strongly articulated opposite position.

Because blatantly unethical conduct should never be condoned or promoted, it is the more frequent subtle compromises with dubious dimensions that permit otherwise ethical practitioners to rationalize their acquiescence. In the shadows of these compromises, we find the personal need for job security, popularity and loyalty trumping ethical behavior.

WHEN RHETORIC CONFRONTS REALITY

Hypothetically, it is easy to say we would never engage in compromise as betrayal. But pragmatically, when confronted with an actual situation where there could or would be serious repercussions, what risks would you be willing to accept?

It is not difficult to give examples of circumstances that might be encountered in healthcare organizations:

- A corporate executive insists on further reducing staff to generate more net income even when such cuts could adversely affect the quality of patient care and services.
- A popular but older surgeon responsible for a substantial volume of admissions is beginning to demonstrate signs of losing his dexterity as reported by the operating room director, but the chief of surgery is adamant that everything is fine.
- An executive involved in merger discussions is financially incentivized to convince the governing body to support the merger when there is no evidence it will benefit the community.
- Two equally compelling proposals are submitted and only one can be funded, but a politically influential physician has a very strong preference.
- A physician responsible for a high volume of patient admissions and hospital revenue may be performing some unnecessary procedures.

Ethical behavior was once described by an English parliamentarian as obedience to the unenforceable. It also has been suggested that the litmus test for ethical behavior is what you do when no one else is looking or would know what you have done. Although wanting to avoid conflict is natural, it should not inhibit proper decision making, as indicated in a previous management ethics column, "Fear of Conflict: Management and Ethical Costs" (Hofmann, P., *Healthcare Executive*, January/February 2012). We become ethically myopic when our personal biases unconsciously prejudice our attitude and behavior. Insight, empathy, perspective and objectivity all fall victim when our hubris denies us the privilege of continuous learning. Consequently, it is not surprising that we also are reluctant to admit and disclose our personal and organizational mistakes. Invariably, there are times when we read but do not understand and hear but do not listen.

In a 2002 column for *The New York Times*, author William Kennedy wrote, "Deceit as a way of life is ubiquitous. Animals hide, mimic, change color, play dead to avoid predators; people disguise themselves, hallucinate, dream, forget and lie to avoid reality, but unlike animals, they also lie to themselves." In the same column, he made reference to a longtime mayor of Albany, New York, who famously said, "I tell the truth whenever I can."

Ethical leaders are those who consistently model organizational values and expected behaviors. At a time when America's favorability view of Congress is poor and once exalted companies have perhaps irreversibly lost their credibility, we should celebrate leaders who are unwilling to make convenient and selfish compromises—those who when conflicted in making a decision are sure to ask the right question. To quote Martin Luther King Jr.:

"Cowardice asks the question, 'Is it safe?' Expedience asks the question, 'Is it politic?' Vanity asks the question, 'Is it popular?' But, conscience asks the question, 'Is it right?'

"And there comes a time when we must take a position that is neither safe, nor politic, nor popular, but one must take it because it is right."

Originally published in the September/October 2016 issue of *Healthcare Executive* magazine.

Discussion Questions

Describe an example of when you felt the personal need for job security, popularity, or loyalty trumped ethical behavior. As a result of this experience, how would you counsel others to avoid such a situation?

Considering your current or future professional role, under what circumstances do you believe it may be ethically justifiable not to tell the truth?

Health Manpower in Underserved Communities

Richard A. Culbertson, PhD

At Louisiana State University's commencement ceremony this past May, I was delighted to see one of my advisees from four years of undergraduate study and four years of medical school receive her medical degree. She aspired to become a rural family physician up to her senior year of medical school. She secured her first choice of residency placement—in vascular surgery at one of the South's leading urban medical centers.

Her choice reflects those available to high-performing students in the highly competitive world of medical education and eventual practice. Yet it also calls attention to a healthcare environment in which stark disparities exist in the burden of disease, availability of professional education and availability of physicians and other healthcare workers. This observation applies both domestically in urban and rural areas and globally between rich and poor nations.

TAKING A CLOSER LOOK

Several explanations for physician and health professional shortages are widely offered, including an absolute shortage of trained personnel. Atul Grover, MD, PhD, executive vice president of the Association of American Medical Colleges, projected a shortage of 150,000 physicians in the present decade despite the opening of new medical schools and expansion of class sizes at existing schools.

This shortage is attributed to increased demand for healthcare services by an aging population, technological and therapeutic advances that make health services more desirable, retirement of existing members of the healthcare workforce and underinvestment in training opportunities—particularly residency slots.

An alternative explanation is that professional shortages reflect a maldistribution of health professionals as opposed to an absolute shortage.

In his article "Health Professionals for a New Century" in the November 29, 2010, issue of *The Lancet,* Julio Frenk, president of the University of Miami, identified professional distribution as a global issue. "Global movements of people, pathogens, technologies, financing, information and knowledge underlie the international transfer of health risks and opportunities," he wrote. "We are increasingly interdependent in terms of key health resources, especially skilled health workers."

The ethical dimensions of the professional distribution problem are severalfold. As medical ethics emerged as a discipline, it was seen in the narrow context of the encounter between the provider and the patient, according to Albert R. Jonsen, PhD, author of the 2003 book *The Birth of Bioethics.*

As the value of healthcare services was increasingly recognized, ethical considerations were extended to public health ethics and the health of broader populations, but typically within a country's borders, according to Nancy E. Kass, ScD, in her 2001 *American Journal of Public Health* article, "An Ethics Framework for Public Health."

This consideration has expanded in recent years to consider global ramifications of health and disease in light of the spread across borders of infectious disease such as Ebola and Zika.

As is often the case in ethical discussions, a balancing of principles is the desired outcome. Utility as a value—that is, the obligation to balance ethical principles in achieving the greatest good for the greatest number—has always been a consideration.

As noted previously, utility often has been narrowly applied when defining the "greatest number," but this view is being challenged as we look to population health as our subject of concern rather than earlier definitions of patients or clients.

The offsetting principle in this case is justice, a principle Michael J. Sandel, author of *Justice: What's the Right Thing to Do?*, argues has only recently received the attention it merits among ethical principles. Justice can be defined as the obligation to act in a fair and impartial manner in making decisions in such areas as the allocation of limited resources and/or services; benefits or burdens; and risks or costs. Its implications for health manpower are clear: Access to skilled personnel at a basic level of proficiency is a key contributor to maintenance of health.

The increasing focus on eliminating health disparities makes it imperative to address the balance of justice and utility.

The principle of respect for persons also applies to addressing the unique health needs of each individual as well as the professional self-determination of those selecting health careers commonly referred to as professional autonomy.

Professionals are expected to abide by the code of ethics of their vocation and to benefit society through service that improves health. In exchange, society has granted professionals freedom in the areas of choice of specialty and practice location based on assessed merit, as noted in the 1990 book *Management of Hospitals and Health Services: Strategic Issues and Performance* by Rockwell Schulz and Alton C. Johnson.

It is exceedingly unlikely that professions in the United States would be forced into coercive practices of mandatory assignment of professionals to underserved areas. This would fly in the face of the free market organization of the U.S. health system and the meritocracy that underpins professional education.

Positive incentives are used to entice healthcare professionals into less-sought-after realms of practice and locations. The establishment of the National Health Services Corps has been a positive step toward addressing access issues in rural and urban areas, as have certain university-sponsored initiatives such as tuition forgiveness for students who commit to practice in underserved areas.

These initiatives are valuable, but they impact only students who practice in health manpower shortage areas, and their benefits sometimes are limited to a specific period of time.

Specialty imbalance in the United States is cited as a contributing factor to shortages of healthcare professionals as an increasing number of these professionals seek more lucrative and lifestyle-friendly specialties than primary care. This observation has applied not only to medicine, but also to advanced practice nursing and allied health professions.

WHERE DO WE GO FROM HERE?

Responses to this problem of distribution have not been successful at the level of residency training to date.

A widely accepted theory in disparities literature holds that patients are often most comfortable and likely to engage in health seeking with professionals of similar ethnic and cultural backgrounds, according to a 2015 Kaiser Family Foundation Issue Brief, *Beyond Health Care: The Role of Social Determinants in Promoting Health and Health Equity*. The discussion of disparities in minority physicians was taking place as far back as at least 1990, when it inspired the Association of American Medical Colleges' "3,000 by 2000" campaign to increase minority enrollment in U.S. schools of medicine to nearly 20 percent of new students. This campaign did not achieve its goal.

A recent initiative has been the deliberate modification of admission practices of medical schools to accept applicants of distinct backgrounds, such as rural upbringing or membership in minority groups, with the desired purpose of the return of these persons as graduate professionals to underserved communities.

A distinct example is the Northern Ontario School of Medicine, which has altered admission requirements, including standard test scores and prerequisites presented by students, to achieve a student body reflecting its rural and often isolated constituents. "It is NOSM's intention to maximize the recruitment of Northern

Ontario students and/or students who have a strong interest in, and aptitude for, practicing medicine in northern urban, rural and remote communities," admissions literature states.

ACHE's *Code of Ethics* calls upon members to "advocate solutions that will improve health status and promote quality healthcare" through public dialogue. Healthcare organizations are taking an increasingly active role in the development of health manpower questions instead of relying on the actions of educational institutions to do so.

A good example is the establishment of a school of medicine by Kaiser Permanente. Set to open in 2019, this school will be devoted to education of physicians versed in population health and oriented toward primary care.

Most organizations do not have resources at this level, but they can offer training opportunities to minority and underserved community providers through funded residencies or training programs. Such initiatives come at a short-term cost to the organization, but they will pay off as society moves toward a model of population health.

Originally published in the November/December 2016 issue of *Healthcare Executive* magazine.

Discussion Questions

Briefly explain why some countries have been more successful in preventing this problem and the ethical relevance for doing so.

Although the COVID-19 pandemic demonstrated that staffing shortages also dramatically affected "well-served" communities, there has been a disproportionate impact on people of color and rural communities. Propose one or two healthcare workforce initiatives beyond those mentioned by the author and describe why they are ethically important.

Asking the Right Questions

Paul B. Hofmann, DrPH, LFACHE

Regular readers of the Sunday edition of *The New York Times* are likely familiar with the column "The Corner Office," written by Adam Bryant, who asks notable CEOs a series of similar questions. The queries frequently include "What were your early years like?" "Any leadership roles for you early on?" "What are some things you've learned about leading and managing people?" and "What kind of career advice do you give to new college grads?"

Over the years, the most intriguing answers for me have been those in response to the dual questions "How do you hire?" and "What questions do you ask?"

SUPPLEMENTING STANDARD QUESTIONS WITH UNPREDICTABLE ONES

Every ACHE member has been a candidate for a number of positions and has no doubt prepared for predictable interview questions, such as: What are your most significant strengths? What are your major weaknesses? How would you describe your leadership style? What is most important to you in a job? What are your career goals? Where would you like to be in five years?

Important but less frequently asked questions can provide insight into a candidate's ethical values and sensitivities. These questions will help determine whether the candidate's moral compass will be compatible with an organization's culture and the senior management staff.

Insights can be acquired by raising a variety of topics. For instance, what do you like most/least in your current position? Give me examples of two or three management mistakes you have made, and share what you learned from them. How many people have you discharged in the past three years, and in retrospect, did you take action later than you should have, or perhaps too soon? Please elaborate. Can you describe a couple of ethical dilemmas you have encountered and how you dealt with them? As you reflect on your work experience to date, what has made you angry in the past? How did you address these issues?

SOME ATYPICAL QUESTIONS POSED BY COMPANY CEOS

The executives interviewed by Bryant offer several provocative questions. For example, Mike Tuchen, CEO, Talend, a software vendor, asks, "What's the hardest problem you've ever solved; why was it hard?"

Drew Houston, CEO, Dropbox, wants to know, "What have you learned in the last year? And if you were able to sit yourself down 10 years ago, what advice would you give your younger self?"

Kathy Giusti, founder, Multiple Myeloma Foundation, asks, "What do you want me to know about you that's not on this résumé?"

Jessica Herrin, founder and CEO, Stella and Dot Family Brands, asks, "What do you want to be known for; what mark do you want to leave?" A favorite question is "Tell me the things that you didn't like about your last job." She added, "When you learn the situations and issues that lead to candidates' dissatisfaction, you can make a relatively accurate judgment about whether they will be able to work in your culture."

Herrin emphasized, "You want to employ optimistic people who are problem solvers, not problem spotters; it's easy for most leadership applicants to analyze what's wrong, but if you come in and say, 'I have an idea; here's something we can do,' she has demonstrated an ability to give you energy rather than take energy from you."

Lloyd Carney, CEO, Brocade, says, "I always ask about the thing you're most proud of and the thing you're least proud of, and sometimes it could be a four-part question, because they'll give something personal and professional for each of them. I'm listening for whether they talk about their accomplishments with 'I, I, I,' or what their team was able to do."

Lori Dickerson Fouché, CEO, Prudential Group Insurance, wants to know, "What kind of cultures do you like to work in? Where do you excel? How do you excel? If you find yourself in situations where they're not going the way you want them to, what do you do?"

Saundra Pelletier, chief executive, WomanCare Global, always asks, "If money, time and talent were no object, and you could be anything at all, what would you be? It's amazing what people will say. I ask about how they act under pressure: Tell me about a stressful situation and give me as many details as you're willing to share. How people behave under real heat tells you a lot about character. I want to know how they're going to fit in our culture. Humility, humor and not taking yourself too seriously are important to me. People who take themselves too seriously are so boring."

Tim Bucher, CEO, Zing Systems, offers this line of questioning: "You've done a lot of things in your life. When you think back on the time that you were the most excited about what you were doing, you couldn't wait to get out of bed and you couldn't shut off at night, what were you doing and why? What I'm really looking for is what makes them tick. The worst answer you can give me is, 'I don't know.'"

Perhaps the most intriguing responses were shared by Stewart Butterfield, cofounder and chief executive, Slack, a communications company. He says, "I used to always ask three short questions—one math, one geography and one history. I didn't expect people to get the answers right, but I just want them to be curious about the world. The first [was] what's three times 17? Then name three countries in Africa. You'd be astonished by the number of people who can't do that. [The third question was] what century was the French Revolution in, give or take 200 years? I don't do that anymore, but I do ask everyone what they want to be when they grow up. Good answers are usually about areas in which they want to grow, things they want to learn, things that they feel like they haven't had a chance to accomplish yet but want to accomplish. A very short answer to that question would be automatically bad."

ASKING PRODUCTIVE INTERVIEW QUESTIONS

All these questions had the same purpose—to determine if these individuals would be a good organizational fit, if their work ethic would match, and if their skill set and values would align with the company's culture. The CEOs knew that their company could not continue to be successful if they did not give the highest priority to making prudent human capital decisions.

The financial and nonfinancial costs of making a poor hiring decision are always higher than expected; once leaders understand that fact, taking the time to hire well is an obvious necessity. As in other fields, every healthcare manager and executive knows that employing the best and the brightest and then giving them the opportunity and freedom to excel are undeniable keys to one's own success as a leader.

Originally published in the September/October 2017 issue of *Healthcare Executive* magazine.

Discussion Questions

Besides all the standard and atypical interview questions described in the article, suggest at least two others that you believe could elicit an expanded impression of a candidate's ethical values.

Every candidate should be familiar with the organization, its leadership, and its history, having obtained this information from a variety of public and perhaps other sources. However, the interviewer will evaluate you in part by the questions you ask—for example, "If I were offered and accepted the position, what is the minimum period I would be expected to stay with the organization?" Recommend two or three additional questions that could give you a sense of the leadership team's moral compass.

The Ethics of Efficiency

Richard A. Culbertson, PhD

THE PURSUIT OF EFFICIENCY through operational improvement has been a goal of managers in all organizational sectors dating back to the beginning of the 20th century and the writings of Frederick Winslow Taylor, a mechanical engineer who sought to improve industrial efficiency. His development of the theory of "scientific management" and the quest for the "one best way" to perform a task based upon observational studies are the stuff of introductory courses in management. One might argue that our current pursuit of evidence-based management finds its roots in this venerable inquiry.

The ACHE *Code of Ethics* states in its preamble that a fundamental objective of the healthcare management profession is to create an "effective and efficient healthcare system." This premise appears so self-evident that it is hard to imagine any objections to a continual striving for greater efficiency as the basis for a managerial philosophy.

The National Academies of Science, Engineering and Medicine in its 2012 report *Best Care at Lower Cost: The Path to Continuously Learning Health Care in America* identified at least 30 percent of medical interventions as being wasteful in nature. More recent surveys of physicians have reached a similar conclusion.

The ethical problem created here features two alternative approaches to efficiency. One is identified as technical efficiency, while the other is allocative efficiency. United Kingdom economists Stephen Palmer and David J. Torgerson define technical efficiency as occurring when the maximum possible improvement is obtained from a set of resources. Most operating decisions made within the sphere of organizational management fall within this definition.

Allocative efficiency takes a broader view of the concept of efficiency, looking at societal effects of resource investment. The National Library of Medicine defines this as assessing competing programs and judging the extent to which they meet objectives. This definition is in keeping with recent emphasis on population health and the impact of a decision on the distribution of health benefits across the community.

ETHICAL FOUNDATIONS OF EFFICIENCY

Technical efficiency is grounded in the ethical principles of beneficence and utility. The simplest application is beneficence, the obligation of the executive to work to the benefit or enhanced well-being of persons served. Utility introduces more explicitly the broader community and evaluates an action in terms of its effects on health rather than intrinsic attributes. It is commonly summarized as the greatest good for the greatest number.

Allocative efficiency derives its ethical basis from the principle of justice. Justice is cited by Kurt Darr, JD, ScD, professor emeritus, hospital administration, Department of Health Services Management and Leadership, Milken Institute School of Public Health, The George Washington University, Washington D.C., as the obligation to act in a fair and impartial manner in making administrative decisions that affect one's institution or any party it serves, such as allocating limited resources and/or services, benefits or burdens, risks and costs.

The task of balancing competing priorities is certainly familiar to practicing executives. The problem comes in electing to concentrate on the simpler question of technical efficiency to the detriment of the broader questions allocative efficiency poses.

A CASE IN POINT: DIAGNOSTIC ACCURACY

Ethical concerns are often illuminated by the use of case examples, which test general principles. A significant problem The National Academies of Science, Engineering and Medicine identifies is that of diagnostic error and its detrimental effects. Danielle Ofri, MD, PhD, an author and physician at Bellevue Hospital, New York, notes in her review of the National Academies 2015 report *Improving Diagnosis in Healthcare* that it contains the "chilling observation that nearly everyone will experience at least one diagnostic error in their lifetimes." They account for an estimated 10 percent of patient deaths, hundreds of thousands of adverse events in hospitals and are a leading cause of paid medical malpractice claims. A diagnostic error might include acid reflux being mistaken for a heart attack, or a pathology report showing cancer that is not communicated to the patient.

Diagnostic error is defined from the perspective of the patient as "the failure to (a) establish an accurate and timely explanation of the patient's health problem(s) or (b) communicate that explanation to the patient." The patient bears the ultimate risk for such errors, as they may lead to improper treatment or to unnecessary interventions. The report goes on to state that "Diagnostic errors may cause harm to patients by preventing or delaying appropriate treatment, providing unnecessary or harmful treatment, or resulting in psychological or financial repercussions." Such errors clearly contradict the beneficence principle of duty to care for the patient above all.

The expert panel that developed the report calls for greater teamwork in the diagnostic process among a range of health professionals, patients and their families. A template for this approach has existed for decades in the rehabilitation sector, but is relatively recent in its application to the acute care setting. Aspiring health professionals are increasingly being educated in team processes and communicating through interprofessional education classwork across disciplinary boundaries.

From the perspective of the executive, the report encourages a work system and culture that support the diagnostic process and improvements in diagnostic performance. Healthcare organizations should promote a nonpunitive environment that values feedback on diagnostic performance.

A controversial issue is the role of information technology in diagnosis. Advocates of the expanded use of IT argue that a major justification for investment in IT is the potential to improve diagnosis and reduce errors. Its critics are concerned that IT does not facilitate the diagnostic process and may even contribute to errors.

BARRIERS TO DIAGNOSTIC IMPROVEMENT

From an ethical perspective, the duty of care for correct diagnosis seems quite clear. Why, then, does this persist as an issue? Perhaps the answer lies in misdirected pursuit of efficiency through limited range of measurement. This is a fundamental problem, for as Clark C. Havighurst, the William Neal Reynolds Professor Emeritus of Law, Duke University, Durham, North Carolina, has stated, "In management, what one measures, one gets."

Efficiency is fundamentally grounded in the ability to measure and then assess improvement. Quality metrics reflect this principle and attempt to construct meaningful measurements that are deemed beneficial to the health of the patient. A prime example is the administration of aspirin to a patient upon arrival in the ED with symptoms of acute myocardial infarction.

Standard quality reporting measures reflect important care processes, but they are proxies for the overall contribution to the health of the patient. They may be selected simply because they are easy to measure. While these are important contributors to a successful outcome, they do not tell the full story.

Another unrelated but compelling concern is that payment systems for hospitals and physicians key off diagnoses, and speed in reaching a diagnosis may facilitate payment. In the effort to achieve a quick diagnosis, accuracy may be sacrificed. This is unfortunate, as the safety expert Pat Croskerry, MD, has observed that "When the diagnosis is made, the thinking stops."

Metrics fail us in the case of diagnostic errors because there is no standard or required way to track them. Robert Berenson, institute fellow at the Urban Institute, Washington, D.C., suggests that this is a result of diagnostic errors being much more difficult to measure than a medication error. The complexity of diagnosis does lend itself to simple measurements.

EFFICIENCY A MEANS TO AN END

Efficiency is a means to an end, in this case the health of the patient, rather than an end in itself. While secondary measures are important, they should not be mistaken for the ultimate goal of enhanced health. Diagnosis is a messy process in many instances rather than an efficient and straightforward one, and it presents an allocative problem for the executive in investing in the problem-solving skills of diagnosis versus investment in new technology.

The ultimate objective, then, is effectiveness in care for which efficiency is a contributor. In the words of legendary University of Minnesota Director/Professor Vernon Weckwerth, PhD, "Efficiency is the number of times the bird flapped its wings, while effectiveness is whether the bird flew."

Originally published in the January/February 2018 issue of *Healthcare Executive* magazine.

Discussion Questions

The author uses the issue of diagnostic errors in medicine to illustrate his basic points. Based on your experience or familiarity with the professional literature in health administration,

(continued)

give an example of when a myopic focus on procedural efficiency eclipsed effectiveness and the ethical costs associated with such a limited focus.

Comment on how one might balance the need for both efficiency and effectiveness to avoid making ethical compromises.

Ethics of Mission and Margin Revisited

Richard A. Culbertson, PhD

In the September/October 2012 issue of *Healthcare Executive*, an article titled "The Ethics of Mission and Margin" was written based on an ACHE program held in conjunction with the San Antonio Cluster in May of that year and led by me.

At that time, I was quoted as identifying the mission versus margin debate as a "conundrum," and continued, "I think margin has been pretty well looked after in the past decade, and as we move into a new health reform era, I would put in a plug for looking at the role of mission—seeing how we can sustain mission in the face of economic challenges." In a 2013 issue of the American Medical Association *Journal of Ethics* devoted to this topic, editor Alessandra Colaianni suggests that "No margin, no mission is too simplistic."

These articles appeared in the flush of optimism that followed the adoption of the Affordable Care Act and the prospect of significant reduction in the burden of uninsured or underinsured patients. With the passage of five years since these publications and a new administration in power, it seems that a current reflection on the ethics of mission and margin is in order to see what ethical issues persist.

MARGIN AND MISSION DEFINED

The expression "No margin, no mission" in healthcare has a history dating to the 1980s in which Sister Irene Kraus, former CEO of the

Daughters of Charity Health System, was said to have popularized the expression. In a 1991 profile in *The New York Times*, her management of the then third largest system in the United States is extolled as exemplary based on operating margin generated by its 36 hospitals and its AA bond rating from Moody's Investor Services. All of this occurred concurrently with a commitment to spend 25 percent of operating income on charitable efforts. Without adequate financial resources to support the provision of high-quality care and the charitable mission, the work of the Daughters would not be sustainable.

The work of the eminent management theorist Peter Drucker also is reflected in the phrase as well. In his book *Managing the Nonprofit Organization*, he writes "There are always so many more moral causes to be served than we have resources for that the nonprofit institution has a duty . . . to allocate its scarce resources for results. . . ." Drucker does not directly address the revenue side of mission management, but certainly speaks directly to the point of efficiency and focus in selecting and managing expenditures.

A CONTROVERSY REIGNITED

A highly anticipated result of the Affordable Care Act was the reduction in the number of uninsured patients that would take place primarily as a result of expansion of the Medicaid program. In the November 17, 2017, *USA Today* article "This Is How the U.S. Has Become a Medicaid Nation," Phil Galewitz of Kaiser Health News describes the wide-ranging and sometimes unanticipated impact of the program's success in reducing numbers of uninsured in states where expansion has been accepted. He notes that Medicaid is the nation's largest health insurance program, covering 74 million Americans. As coverage is episodic, 25 percent of Americans will be on Medicaid during the course of a year as a result of changes in employment and earnings.

Public health advocates argue that the benefits of expansion have been substantial with regard to earlier detection of disease and heightened utilization of preventive and primary care services. As an example, a report by Jim Richardson, PhD, of the LSU Public Administration Institute, credits Medicaid expansion in Louisiana with an additional 35,733 breast cancer screenings, resulting in 338 confirmed diagnoses; and 48,482 adults receiving specialized outpatient mental health services. From an ethical perspective, this is a beneficence for the population as a whole.

Yet it is also argued that Medicaid expansion has reduced access to care as physicians and provider organizations are overwhelmed by increased demand for services, resulting in reduced access to care in certain areas. Julia Paradise of the Kaiser Family Foundation notes that while 70 percent of physicians nationally accept new Medicaid patients, there is a distinct range from 39 percent in New Jersey to 97 percent in Nebraska. She also reports that 85 percent accept new commercially insured patients, and that rates vary by specialty.

From the perspective of the healthcare executive responsible for the financial health of the organization, the substitution of compensated patients for uninsured is clearly beneficial. However, Peter Ubel suggests in *Forbes* magazine that on average Medicaid pays 61 percent of Medicare rates (subject to regional variation), which is in turn lower than commercial insurers' payment. The strategy of attracting more highly insured patients at the exclusion of others is a widely employed strategy. Even safety-net public hospitals seek to partially solve the "no margin, no mission" conundrum by offering services that will attract highly insured patients to their doors.

WHICH APPROACH IS ETHICALLY PREFERABLE?

Health economist Paul Feldstein of the University of California–Irvine devised a model of patient composition of physician practice by payer category. In a rational economic world, a physician would progress from the most to least remunerative payer categories and close her or his practice to the lesser categories once available practice time could be filled. Thus, physicians who could fill their appointment books with cash, commercial insurance and managed care patients would close their practices to Medicare and Medicaid patients.

Numerous medical schools have adopted graduation oaths in which new medical doctors pledge to see all patients regardless of "economic standing or ability to pay," which is a portion of the physician oath at Tulane School of Medicine. This is a laudable aspiration, but one that experienced practice managers such as Frederick Wenzel and Jane M. Wenzel, PhD, would caution needs to be balanced against available revenues.

ETHICAL GUIDANCE FROM THE ACHE *CODE OF ETHICS*

In the ACHE *Code of Ethics*, there is a clear mandate for the healthcare executive to "Work to support access to healthcare services for all people." There also is an obligation to "Provide healthcare services consistent with available resources," and in the event of limited resources, "work to ensure the existence of a resource allocation process that considers ethical ramifications."

There also is an admonition to ensure that the executive's organization will engage in "sound business practices." Given the scope of healthcare organizations' multipronged missions of patient care, community service and, in many cases, teaching and research, it is common practice to seek to maximize returns from patient care to subsidize losses in the other mission elements.

The *Code of Ethics* also articulates a duty of veracity on the part of the executive. The executive is to "Be truthful in all forms of organizational communication, and avoid disseminating information that is false, misleading, or deceptive."

The German philosopher Immanuel Kant identified truth telling as an absolute imperative of duty-based ethics. In his system, the obligation to truth telling is immutable and tolerates no exception. This maxim still is invoked in bioethics with regard to patient autonomy and the caregiver's obligation to provide truthful information to the patient as reflected in the AMA *Code of Ethics*.

Yet there is another duty of the healthcare executive posed in the ACHE *Code of Ethics* and that is to "Encourage and participate in public dialogue on healthcare policy issues, and advocate solutions that will improve health status and support quality healthcare." As the future of the ACA and the accompanying expansion of Medicaid in many states are the subject of intense political debate, bringing the issue of margin versus mission to public scrutiny is a responsible step.

Lacking full information, policymakers and the public may assume that all is well with institutional and professional providers, and that any loss of covered patients can be easily absorbed by these providers in the near term. It is likely, therefore, that pressure to optimize payer mix will only grow. The ethically responsible course is to bring the issue into public debate rather than withhold the unpleasant realities.

Originally published in the May/June 2018 issue of *Healthcare Executive* magazine.

Discussion Questions

The Affordable Care Act expanded Medicaid coverage for most low-income adults to 138 percent of the federal poverty level, but as of April 2020, 14 states had yet to participate and the number of physicians accepting Medicaid patients varies widely from state to state. When promoting public debate and supporting lobbying efforts, what ethical arguments can be used to improve the situation affecting both hospitals and physicians?

Discuss briefly why you are hopeful or pessimistic about short- and long-term strategies for dealing with this challenge.

Obligations to the Community

William A. Nelson, PhD, HFACHE,
and Lauren A. Taylor, PhD

Recently, many Americans have publicly become more politically and socially active, and healthcare professionals are no exception. Public activism raises the question of what obligations, if any, do healthcare executives have in taking a position on issues regarding the delivery of healthcare and health promotion?

Insight into this question lies within the context of ACHE's *Code of Ethics*. As a condition of membership to ACHE, all members agree to adhere to the *Code of Ethics*. As noted in the ACHE web-based ethics toolkit, "ACHE believes the *Code* is integral to the practice of healthcare management." The *Code* serves as the standard to guide members' ethical decisions and actions. The *Code*, following a preamble, contains a breakdown of professional responsibilities to patients, the organization, employees, and the profession, and a substantive section on responsibilities to community and society. Within the context of the healthcare executive's responsibilities to community and society are five specific obligations. This is a powerful component of the *Code*, calling executives to examine their own and their organization's values and commit to taking a role in social responsibility.

Each specific obligation to the community and society is deserving of executives' renewed consideration and self-examination. The *Code* does not direct what members should think, but what members should be thinking about. We briefly highlight this aspect of the *Code of Ethics* and offer some practical comments related to the specific obligations.

REFLECTIONS ON THE RESPONSIBILITIES TO COMMUNITY AND SOCIETY

"Work to identify and meet the healthcare needs of the community." The statement is clear and meaningful for leaders of healthcare organizations. They are responsible for understanding the community's needs and seeking to meet them. If leaders are going to meet the community's needs, it's important to fully understand what those needs are.

"Work to support access to healthcare services for all people." This requirement also seems to be fairly routine, although it does raise questions about how far must the work of executives go to support the access of healthcare services to all people. Should healthcare executives be involved in lobbying legislatures, for instance, for the expansion of Medicaid or other types of insurance? To date, healthcare advocacy organizations, such as the American Hospital Association and several state-based hospital associations, have generally lined up behind Medicaid expansion, viewing it as having an impact on the bottom line if Medicaid payments replace uncompensated care. But we know that health insurance is only one step toward meaningful access to healthcare. Millions of low-income people, many of whom are insured by Medicaid, are searching for mental healthcare in a system in which many individual providers accept only commercial or out-of-pocket payments.

"Encourage and participate in public dialogue on healthcare policy issues and advocate solutions that will improve health status and promote quality healthcare." Herein, the *Code of Ethics* calls upon executives to take an active stance as citizens on

a potentially wide range of policy issues not only related to the delivery of healthcare but also health promotion. Current attention to social determinants of health underscores that relevant domains of healthcare and health policy may span housing, nutrition, transportation and zoning.

Hosting communitywide meetings and events on healthcare campuses may be one way to fulfill this part of the *Code*. Another may be taking on a more deliberate community organizing role in soliciting community input on federally mandated community health needs assessments. Even though ACHE does not advocate as an organization, the *Code of Ethics* calls members to individually consider the scope of their obligations. Although some executives may feel uncomfortable publicly expressing their own healthcare-related policy views, publicly advocating for policies that are aligned with the organization's mission, vision and values is a given. When in doubt, executives may rightly convene others to share their views and simply sit and listen.

"Apply short- and long-term assessments to management decisions affecting both community and society." Such a standard carries an implicit requirement that administrators are able to ascertain the short- and long-term impacts of their choices on community and society. Doing so may be challenging given the far-reaching ripple effects of healthcare executives' decisions. For instance, healthcare executives' advocacy for health insurance expansion may be expected to deliver short-term expansions in access but may negatively impact the availability of public resources that could be committed to other social priorities. The full range of all impacts from a given action may not be understood, but making a habit of looking beyond quarterly and yearly time horizons can help executives meet this standard.

"Provide prospective patients and others with adequate and accurate information, enabling them to make enlightened

decisions regarding services." This standard raises provocative questions about the extent to which healthcare executives are obligated to provide prospective patients with information about costs and quality of recommended treatments, which in many markets is not standard practice. Moreover, administrators may ask themselves what defines prospective patients. Are these only people who walk through the front doors of the clinic, office or hospital for assessment, or are they a larger set of people who might never consider receiving services?

FINAL THOUGHTS

This brief review of the ACHE *Code of Ethics* supports the understanding that healthcare executives have significant social responsibilities that parallel, and in some sense exceed, those of physicians. Dating back to the establishment of the ACHE *Code of Ethics* in 1941, healthcare executives have been expected to be leaders not only within their organizations but also in their communities and society.

To satisfy this important ethical standard, healthcare executives need to be well informed and possess accurate information about the many issues impacting the delivery of healthcare and the ability to foster the health of the community. Armed with current information, executives must reflect on their own perspectives on how best to support the access of healthcare for all people or their position on various healthcare policy issues. Available information will often be insufficient or inconclusive, in which case executives must be prepared to rely on the organization's mission and values in decision making. In anticipation of such difficult choices, healthcare executives would be wise to explore these issues with other employees and stakeholders.

Of course, there are risks with public engagement in that some people may either disagree with your perspective or think you are overstepping your role. However, we believe the *Code* calls on healthcare executives not to be silent concerning important issues. The voice of the executive in the public dialogue is crucial. ACHE's *Code of Ethics* calls on executives to examine their own and their organization's values and commit to taking a role in social responsibility.

Originally published in the September/October 2018 issue of *Healthcare Executive* magazine.

Discussion Questions

The authors highlight a variety of actions healthcare executives can take to fulfill their organization's social responsibilities to its community and to society. Given the pivotal roles of the governing body and medical staff, offer some additional ethically grounded actions an executive might take to engage them in the process.

In view of the rapidly growing appreciation for the importance of population health management and the social determinants of health, what other steps could executives take to address these issues, beyond those mentioned by the authors?

Updated Ethics Self-Assessment Addresses Current Issues

Sinde A. Hahn, FACHE, CAE

HEALTHCARE LEADERS BELONG TO a field in which ethics are paramount. As the professional home for healthcare executives, ACHE has woven an ethics-focused culture into the fabric of our organization.

Our *Code of Ethics* is a defining document for the organization, our members and the profession; so much so that the *Code* is a requirement of ACHE membership.

The Ethics Self-Assessment is an invaluable tool available to ACHE members. Based on the *Code of Ethics*, the self-assessment is used to evaluate leadership and ethics-related actions, and to address potential red flags identified in the process.

The self-assessment gives life to the *Code of Ethics* and functions as a checklist of best practices in different areas. Perhaps more importantly, the assessment provides a framework for individuals to evaluate the frequency of their own action in demonstrating ethical behaviors and in relationship with others.

Each year, ACHE's Ethics Committee reviews and considers revisions to the Ethics Self-Assessment. Typically, these revisions consist of minor changes, but in 2018, the committee added eight new statements to better reflect some of the larger issues at stake in healthcare today. Following are summaries of the issues that prompted the revisions.

Recent Additions and Changes to the Ethics Self-Assessment:

- I take responsibility for understanding workplace violence and take steps to eliminate it.
- I engage in collaborative efforts with healthcare organizations, businesses, elected officials and others to improve the community's well-being.
- I seek to identify, understand and eliminate health disparities in my community.
- I seek to understand and identify the social determinants of health in my community.
- I am committed to eliminating harm in the workplace.
- I am committed to helping address affordability challenges in healthcare.
- I am sensitive to the stress of the healthcare workforce (including physicians and other clinicians), and take steps to address personal wellness and professional fulfillment, such as incorporating these issues in employee and physician satisfaction/engagement surveys.
- I take steps to understand my workforce as it relates to safety, stress and burnout, and consider the impact of those who are in positions of authority (including executives and physicians).

WORKPLACE VIOLENCE

The only change within the leadership category pertains to an executive's responsibility to understand workplace violence and take steps to eliminate it. The addition of this statement stems from increased violence in the workplace.

COMMUNITY HEALTH

Three new statements were added to the community section of the relationships category to better reflect that healthcare organizations are responsible for the health of the communities they serve.

PATIENT SAFETY

In the section pertaining to patients and their families, the committee introduced two new statements related to articulating executive commitment to eliminate harm in the workplace and address affordability challenges in healthcare.

BURNOUT

Finally, the committee added two new statements under the colleagues and staff subcategory to focus on the need for greater awareness of stress among the workforce—including the impact of those in positions of authority—and to take steps to address the personal wellness and professional fulfilment of employees and physicians.

ACHE is committed to supporting its members and the important work they do with tools like the Ethics Self-Assessment, *Code of Ethics* and other resources that comprise the ACHE Ethics Toolkit. Visit ache.org/EthicsToolkit to access these resources.

Originally published in the July/August 2019 issue of *Healthcare Executive* magazine.

Discussion Questions

The self-assessment tool is located at ache.org/EthicsToolkit. After reviewing the self-assessment tool, what role do you see it playing in healthcare organizations?

(continued)

Describe how a healthcare executive may consider using the ACHE self-assessment tool to enhance communication during performance reviews.

Revisiting the Executive's Role in Malpractice Cases

Paul B. Hofmann, DrPH, LFACHE

In a previous column ("The Executive's Role in Malpractice Cases," *Healthcare Executive*, May/June 2008), I noted that despite impressions to the contrary, it is anger and not greed that drives most malpractice lawsuits. Since that time, I have continued to serve as an expert witness for both defense and plaintiff attorneys. Although there are still too many instances when clinical mistakes are denied, timely disclosures and apologies are not made, results of investigations are not shared and compensation offers are not extended, more hospitals are taking a less adversarial position.

We are aware of the following:

1. Medical errors are reportedly the third leading cause of death in the U.S.
2. Most preventable medical errors are not the result of individual ineptitude, but are instead acts of omission or commission by fallible people (physicians, nurses, pharmacists and others) or are due to a system failure.
3. Clinically competent physicians (often along with the hospital) are sometimes sued following an adverse clinical outcome attributable to poor communication skills and a lack of responsiveness to patient/family concerns.

4. Many patients are unaware of preventable errors that occur, such as hospital-acquired infections.
5. Some physicians who do not produce optimal clinical outcomes avoid lawsuits because of a long relationship with their patients and an exemplary bedside manner. According to a February 20, 2019, report by the nonprofit Physicians Advocacy Institute, 44 percent of physicians were employed by hospitals in January 2018, compared to just one in four in July 2012, increasing the potential liability exposure for these organizations.

Disturbing Findings in a Recent Study

A special article in the March 28, 2019, issue of the *New England Journal of Medicine* titled "Changes in Practice Among Physicians with Malpractice Claims" noted that over 480,000 physicians were responsible for almost 69,000 paid claims from 2003 through 2015. The article cited that 89 percent had no claims, 8.8 percent had one claim and the remaining 2.3 percent accounted for 38.9 percent of all the other claims. The authors analyzed the associations between the number of paid malpractice claims the physicians accrued, the number of exits from medical practice, changes in clinical volume, changes in geographic relocation and a change in practice group size.

The article noted that the "overwhelming majority of doctors who had five or more paid claims [continued to practice]. And they also moved to solo practice and small groups more often, where there's even less oversight, so these problematic doctors may produce even worse outcomes." Although the physicians who accumulated more claims were more likely to stop practicing, over 90 percent who had at least five claims were still in practice and twice as likely as those with fewer claims to go into solo practice.

(continued)

Nearly one-third of the claims were related to patient deaths and close to one-half were related to major or significant non-fatal injury. Because of this, it is reasonable to assume that a substantial proportion of these claims, which were either settled or went to trial, involved a hospital as a co-defendant with a "deeper pocket" (i.e., more insurance coverage than the physician). Fortunately, the creation of the National Practitioner Data Bank has presumably reduced the ability of incompetent physicians to move across state lines to avoid detection. However, the NPDB is not flawless and state medical boards vary in their level of performance.

Based on my experience as an expert witness in over 25 states, I can confirm that there are remarkable performance variations in the following:

- Formal oversight of physicians with multiple malpractice claims
- Willingness of hospitals to limit or suspend the privileges of a physician responsible for a large volume of admissions, representing significant institutional revenue
- Compliance with well-written and appropriate hospital policies
- Efficacy of medical staff credentialing processes
- Inclination of the hospital or medical staff to intercede when a physician is exhibiting physical or mental health problems

RECOMMENDATIONS

Those of us in executive positions have an inherent responsibility to ensure the safety of patients and to improve the quality of care provided by our organizations. Our clinical colleagues, governing bodies and the communities we serve must demand no less.

Key steps for hospital executives dedicated to reducing malpractice include:

1. ***Become more vigilant, regardless of organization size.*** There is a misconception that rural and smaller hospitals are at a higher risk of malpractice suits. This isn't necessarily the case. Though these organizations are vulnerable, consider the example of a prominent medical center that made headlines earlier this year when there was undeniable evidence of inexplicable and unusually bad outcomes for pediatric patients receiving cardiac surgery, which were not simply isolated incidents. Regrettably, timely action was not taken despite such evidence, and the institution along with physicians were sued.
2. ***Strengthen your organization's credentialing procedures, focusing on the processes for new applicants and candidates for reappointment.*** Give particular attention to the latter's complication rates, other adverse outcomes, excessive lengths of patient stays and readmission rates.
3. ***Assess unusual utilization patterns.*** In a Washington state malpractice case, an OB-GYN was determined to be performing an inordinate number of hysterectomies, resulting in substantial revenue for a small community hospital. Disturbingly, over 25 percent of the procedures involved women under the age of 30. Even though the majority of the resulting jury award went against the physician, 35 percent was allocated to the hospital for the medical staff's failure to recognize and halt the surgeon's excessive operations.

4. ***Adopt the six measures proposed in 2017 by the ACHE and the IHI Lucian Leape Institute***
   - Establish a compelling vision for safety
   - Build trust, respect and inclusion
   - Select, develop and engage the board
   - Prioritize safety in selection and development of leaders
   - Lead and reward a Just Culture
   - Establish organizational behavior expectations

Everyone who has the privilege of working in a hospital must be a patient advocate, regardless of his or her position, but members of senior management should be particularly committed to fully supporting medical staff efforts to identify and reduce physician malpractice. Our patients will obviously be the ultimate beneficiaries.

Originally published in the September/October 2019 issue of *Healthcare Executive* magazine.

Discussion Questions

Provide your thoughts about additional reasons that marginally competent physicians are still permitted to practice without proper oversight.

Describe one or two other steps executives might take to reduce malpractice that demonstrate their implicit ethical obligation to ensure all patients receive safe and high-quality care.

Duty to Care

William A. Nelson, PhD, HFACHE,
and Raina H. Jain, MD

Soon after the early reports of rapidly spreading COVID-19 infections, hospitals throughout the United States and beyond began reviewing their emergency preparedness guidelines. With the realization that COVID-19 was becoming a pandemic, public health officials and institutional leaders recognized the need to prepare for an influx of COVID-19 patients that would challenge an institution's ability to deliver its standard of care.

A March 16 report from The Hastings Center (*Ethical Framework for Health Care Institutions & Guidelines for Institutional Ethics Services Responding to the Coronavirus Pandemic*) called on institutional leaders' pandemic preparations to focus on three fundamental obligations: to plan (manage uncertainty); guide (draft guidelines to address the potential disruption to standard healthcare); and safeguard (healthcare providers and vulnerable populations). Leaders can learn from a review of how these preparations were set into motion at the start of the COVID-19 crisis, and determine their implications for future crises.

LEADERSHIP'S DUTY TO PLAN

At the start of the COVID-19 pandemic, healthcare leaders recognized their responsibility to plan, constructing various approaches involving administrative and clinical leaders, ethicists, and legal counsel to ensure preparedness plans would be developed in the context of an ethical framework. There was a potential need to shift an institution's focus from the care of individual patients to the allocation of limited resources in an effort to optimize health outcomes for the population as a whole. Preparing for this scenario necessitated particularly thoughtful planning.

LEADERSHIP'S DUTY TO GUIDE

To help manage uncertainty related to the public health emergency, institutions developed guidelines to prepare for potential challenges. As noted in The Hastings Center report, the tension between equality and equity, expressed through the fair allocation of limited resources, "is stark when life-sustaining interventions are not available to all patients who could benefit from these interventions." In an effort to address such ethical conflicts, institutions across the United States drafted allocation guidelines designed to ration scarce resources if a surge of critically ill patients necessitated the need to distribute critical resources, including staff and ICU beds, and supplies, such as ventilators and medications. The fundamental purpose of such guidelines has been to maximize the number of lives saved and to prevent suffering while protecting the equitable worth of every person.

LEADERSHIP'S DUTY TO SAFEGUARD STAFF

Equally central to planning and guiding during the pandemic is an organization's responsibility to manage the use of employees as a resource while safeguarding their health. This is particularly important, given that the COVID-19 virus is highly contagious with significant associated morbidity and mortality. Notably, the ability of leadership to manage the allocation of employees hinges on healthcare professionals' ethical duty to provide care even with a heightened risk of harm.

As the pandemic continues, some healthcare providers have questioned their professional responsibility to provide care for infected patients when their actions have implications for themselves and their loved ones. There has been concern about the expectations of medical providers of all ages—from older primary care physicians with their own underlying health conditions to newly minted medical school graduates—to serve when their own health might be at risk. In attempting to fulfill the beneficence-based ethical obligation to provide patient care despite potential risks, however, healthcare leaders should also acknowledge ethically justifiable limits to providers' duties to serve. Such limits are covered in an April 15 article in the journal *Academic Medicine* titled "Teaching Professional Formation in Response to the COVID-19 Pandemic." The authors describe "the professional virtue of self-sacrifice, which creates the ethical obligation to accept only reasonable risks to oneself to fulfill beneficence-based ethical obligations to patients." They continue, "it is essential that the judgment of reasonableness [of risk] be made in a disciplined way."

In the case of the COVID-19 pandemic, the consideration of adequate personal protective equipment is crucial to distinguishing between reasonable and unreasonable risk, and between recklessness and heroism. An analogy can be drawn in considering the role of a firefighter, who would not be expected to rush into a burning building without personal protection.

While many institutions have drafted guidelines to ensure adequate staffing to treat patients, such guidelines must be balanced with an equivalent obligation to ensure staff safety through necessary infection control supplies and protocols for patient engagement. Without such preparation and protection, the risk undertaken by healthcare professionals may be considered unreasonable and thus exempt from an ethical obligation to serve.

Two additional areas of focus necessary for safeguarding healthcare professionals need to be captured in institutional guidelines.

Healthcare professionals should be assured when needing to implement approved triage protocols that they will be protected from legal liability. Without such protections, the implementation of the triage guidelines can be impaired. Providing effective emotional support for front-line staff is another important component of safeguarding staff. The need to ration resources, including withholding or withdrawing ventilators, can cause disabling moral distress for some clinicians. Institutional guidelines cannot necessarily prevent such stress during the pandemic or other emergencies; however, strategies to reduce long-term moral injury are essential.

PREPARING FOR FUTURE EMERGENCIES

The institutional responsibility to plan, guide and safeguard persists through the course of this pandemic, as it was in prior and will be in future public health emergencies. It is not an easy task because COVID-19 is wrought with ethical challenges. To address them, institutional guidelines need to be ethically grounded and clear and include transparent triage protocols to save the most lives while being fair and equitable in resource distribution. As the COVID-19 pandemic eventually eases its grip on every aspect of society, crisis management guidelines need to be assessed. Leaders should ask questions about their organizations' guidelines, including: Did they achieve patient care goals? Did the ethical principles that guide healthcare professionals' duty to care conflict with the institution's failure to adequately safeguard employees? Leadership needs to recognize healthcare workers' ability to appropriately fulfill their ethically grounded roles and responsibilities is dependent on administrators' ability to adequately fulfill their own role of creating a safe environment.

Originally published in the September/October 2020 issue of *Healthcare Executive* magazine.

Discussion Questions

Describe how the ethical tension can be reduced when making decisions that prioritize optimizing health outcomes for the community rather than for individual patients.

If some staff members express reluctance to jeopardize their health and potentially the health of family members during a pandemic, how should supervisors and management respond?

An Executive-Driven Ethical Culture

William A. Nelson, PhD, HFACHE,
and John J. Donnellan Jr., FACHE

AN ORGANIZATION'S CULTURE PLAYS a significant role in providing an identity to staff members and shaping their behavior. The culture encompasses many elements, including shared values and beliefs, implicit and patterned assumptions that influence staff decisions, and observable characteristics such as dress, rituals, and communication. Culture is a key driver in establishing and maintaining an ethical organization because of its effect on staff members' actions.

An ethics-grounded culture needs to be a top priority for healthcare executives because of its importance to quality care and, ultimately, the organization's success overall. The culture can never be taken for granted and may need periodic renewal.

Today's healthcare executives should review, reflect, and, when needed, foster changes to their organizations' cultures. Conduct an honest, systematic review of your own executive behaviors and your organization's ethical culture. This can be done by using ACHE's Ethics Self-Assessment, available in the Ethics area of **ache.org** and once a year in *Healthcare Executive*, and by talking openly and honestly with your organization's ethics committee, senior leadership, and staff. You may be persuaded of the need for cultural change.

Improving the ethical culture is not easy, it takes time, and it will not happen by accident. It requires thoughtful, dedicated focus that actively involves healthcare leadership. There are fundamental components of an institution's culture—mission/vision/

values; organizational structure, including a formal ethics program; and leadership behavior—that can address these issues and serve as building blocks for an organization's ethical framework.

MISSION, VISION, VALUES

A healthcare organization must begin by establishing or reviewing the statement of values upon which the organization's mission and vision are grounded. Those values must be clearly communicated to all employees early and often, beginning with the interviewing process, reinforced during employee orientation and regularly acknowledged during performance reviews, public ceremonies, celebrations, and awards. The statement of values should reflect the organization's commitment to integrity, transparency, and safety, in addition to quality and efficiency.

The mission, vision, and values cannot be simply words in a document. The document should meet the expectation of all staff members. In addition, employee position descriptions and performance evaluations need to be aligned with organizational values. For example, the organization should place an emphasis on error reporting, patient disclosure, and identification of safety vulnerabilities that is equal to the emphasis it places on achieving quality, utilization, and financial targets. Staff should be acknowledged, rewarded, and celebrated when behaviors exemplify organizational values. Leaders of healthcare organizations should consider celebrating actions taken by individuals or units that may not have achieved an intended objective but that exemplify an unwavering adherence to the organization's values.

MISSION, VISION, AND VALUES CHECKLIST

- Have your mission, vision, and values been recently updated?

- Are all employees aware of the organization's mission, vision, and values?
- Are the mission, vision, and values integrated into all employees' position descriptions and performance reviews?
- Do clinical and administrative decisions reflect the organization's mission, vision, and values?

AN EFFECTIVE ETHICS PROGRAM

Healthcare executives must ensure that an effective formal ethics program infrastructure exists to both proactively promote ethical practices and clarify ethical uncertainty when needed. The ethics program should be system oriented and integrated into daily life at the organization.

The ethics mechanism should be available to address a broad array of issues beyond clinical questions. For example, it should have the capacity to address questions about resource allocation, organizational strategy, and community mission. Executives should not only support ethics programs but openly use them in their decision making.

The challenge to leadership is to align the activities of the organization's ethics program or committee with the organization's values and other programs, such as patient safety and quality improvement. The ethics program should be made clear to patients, staff, stakeholders, trustees, and the community served and should be responsive to their needs.

Executives need to support training of members of the organization's ethics program. And ethics program leaders in turn should provide educational offerings to staff, patients, and trustees that are designed to reinforce organizational values, teach ways to resolve situations in which a conflict between observed behaviors and institutional values occurs, and discuss, through the use of actual case studies, how ethical conflicts were brought forward and addressed in the organization.

EFFECTIVE ETHICS PROGRAM CHECKLIST

- Does leadership openly and publicly support the ethics program?
- Are ethics activities integrated into the organization?
- Have ethics committee members been trained to address clinical and organization issues?
- Do all staff members have access to the ethics program?
- Are recurring ethical issues identified and addressed?
- Is staff moral distress acknowledged and addressed at every level in the organization?

EXECUTIVE ACTION

The final component in building an ethical culture is having administrative and clinical leaders demonstrate an unwavering commitment to the importance of ethics. Linda Trevino, PhD, of the Pennsylvania State University, noted in a 2005 presentation that executive ethical leadership includes the leader's behavior (moral person)—including traits, personal morality, and values-based decision making—and the leader's ability to direct followers' behavior (moral manager), including role modeling and how the leader rewards and disciplines and communicates the importance of ethics.

Being a model for ethical behaviors is set in day-to-day actions and decisions. Lynn Sharp Paine, in a 1994 *Harvard Business Review* article (vol. 72, no. 2), challenged managers to "acknowledge their role in sharpening organizational ethics and seize this opportunity to create a climate that can strengthen the relationships and reputations on which their companies' success depends." Paine argues the need for organizations to design an ethical framework that is ". . . no longer a burdensome constraint . . . but the governing ethos of the organization."

A key component in role modeling is openly discussing ethics and using the organization's ethics resources. When managerial performance targets are being determined or resource allocation and financial strategy is being decided, are the decisions made within the context of organizational values? When executive leadership establishes and embarks on new capital and strategic projects, such as an expansion of radiation oncology or the construction of a new emergency facility, is the decision reached using an ethically guided decision-making process? Or is it considered simply in the framework of a business decision? The use of an ethically guided decision-making process will assist the organization when making a public announcement about the decision and answering questions that inevitably will be raised about lost opportunities (e.g., not to pursue expansion of home- and community-based services).

It is easy to publicly proclaim how decisions are reached following a process that ensures consistency with values. However, the true test of a leader's adherence to organizational values often comes in the most difficult of times—for example, the leader's willingness to publicly disclose activities such as fraudulent reporting, billing inaccuracies, or safety violations. The Joint Commission requires healthcare organizations to conduct intensive investigations of actual or potential system failures that harm or might have harmed patients. Is leadership willing to take the additional step of widely disclosing the error, the analysis, and the findings?

ETHICS LEADERSHIP CHECKLIST

- Do clinicians' and administrative executives' actions reflect adherence to the organization's values?
- Does leadership openly talk about the importance of ethics?
- Are executive decision-making processes and decisions transparent?
- Do healthcare executives consult with the organization's ethics committee?

- Do healthcare executives serve as role models regarding ethical behavior and traits?

An ethics-driven culture is central to quality care. When unethical behaviors or even ethical uncertainty exists, the quality of care can be diminished. Staff members are demoralized and less effective. The organization's culture is a complex dynamic that has evolved over time and includes both formal (policies, staff selection, decision processes, etc.) and informal (rituals, dress, daily employee relations and behavior, language, etc.) systems.

Healthcare executives play a key role in setting the tone for building, maintaining, and, when needed, changing policies so the organization's culture becomes more grounded in ethics. Just as the current culture did not happen by accident or overnight, enhancing the culture will not just happen by chance—it requires attention, thoughtful review, careful planning, and clear leadership. The benefits to an organization of having an ethical culture make the effort worth it.

Originally published in the November/December 2009 issue of *Healthcare Executive* magazine.

Discussion Questions

The authors emphasize the importance of an executive-driven ethical culture for organizational success and quality care. What metrics should healthcare executives use to determine that their organization has an ethically grounded culture?

A central component in building an ethical culture is having administrative and clinical leaders openly and consistently demonstrate an unwavering commitment to the importance of ethics and professionalism. Identify several barriers that leaders must overcome to achieve their goal of an ethically grounded culture.

Confronting Management Incompetence

Paul B. Hofmann, DrPH, LFACHE

Too many executives do not deal in a timely way with incompetent or marginally competent managers. Why is this an ethics issue and how should it be addressed?

In healthcare, as in every field, one of the most fundamental and challenging responsibilities of a leader is to tackle tough and uncomfortable situations promptly and effectively. If an otherwise very capable executive has only one shortcoming, it will often be the failure to move decisively when a senior officer, department head, or supervisor is performing poorly.

Failing to take action constitutes a grave ethical lapse. Staff morale suffers when incompetence is tolerated and even rewarded. Unfortunately, depending on their area of responsibility, incompetent managers eventually compromise patient care, subordinates, peers, and possibly the organization itself. Furthermore, failing to address this issue harms the executive's moral authority to lead.

Ironically, the ineffectiveness of a particular manager is rarely a secret. Subordinates are certainly aware of the problem, as are peers and others who must contend with this person's inadequate performance. Ineffectual managers themselves are usually aware of their deficiencies, although they may have difficulty admitting the need for improvement.

Remarkably, executives may not fully appreciate that their own position is at risk. If inferior performance is tolerated for an extended period, leadership's credibility inevitably will be adversely affected. Key members of the organization will raise legitimate questions: Does senior management know there is a problem? If it does, why is nothing being done? If an executive does not realize a manager is not performing well, why not?

REASONS FOR PROCRASTINATION

Assuming that performance problems of an ineffective manager are known and irreversible, there are a number of reasons why they may not be addressed in a suitable manner:

1. Confronting this issue is hardly enjoyable; indeed, it is the least pleasant part of management and is not usually covered in either undergraduate or graduate courses.
2. Conceding that you may have made a bad hiring or promotion decision will always be hard.
3. Resolving a management performance predicament can consume a significant amount of time and emotional energy.
4. Maintaining the status quo is easier and avoids the uncertainty associated with changes.
5. Overcoming inertia is especially difficult if the person is well liked, hardworking, loyal, and conscientious; supports a large family; is within a few years of retirement; has "political" connections; and/or received consistently acceptable performance reviews from prior supervisors.
6. Hoping the individual will still meet clearly agreed on expectations, despite a previous inability to do so, is an illusion that can be rationalized easily.

When interviewing candidates for a senior executive position, among the questions I routinely asked was, "How many people have you terminated in the past five years, and, if you could do it again, would you have handled those decisions any differently?" Typically, one person would say, "I did not terminate anyone; everybody is salvageable." Another might think for a short period and then reply, "I fired four people, it had to be done, and I wouldn't have changed a thing." Invariably, a third candidate would respond, "I had to discharge three, and it was painfully difficult, but perhaps I waited too long." While extending a job offer obviously was not solely dependent on their answers to these questions, this part of the interview conversation always contributed to a better understanding of the candidate's management style and philosophy.

RECOMMENDATIONS

Among other attributes, managing ethically requires competency, courage, and compassion. Assuming again that every reasonable step has been taken to help the individual improve his or her performance to no avail and another more suitable position is not available, each of these attributes is particularly relevant in dealing successfully with a manager whose performance is unacceptable.

Competency in this context means the executive does not rationalize, procrastinate, or naively underestimate the organizational cost of incompetence. Instead, when there is no doubt action must be taken, a comprehensive plan must be carefully prepared. This plan may include

- consultation with legal counsel, human resources, and key people within the organization;
- reviewing documentation of progressive disciplinary action to assure the individual has been properly counseled and to defend an allegation of wrongful discharge;
- consultation with the board and medical staff leaders;

- verification that contractual obligations will be met and severance benefits are accurately determined;
- consideration of additional benefits, such as assistance with job placement; and
- preparation of internal and possibly external announcements, including designation of an interim manager.

Unquestionably, other issues should be considered, but creating and implementing a detailed plan will maximize the likelihood that the transition will be responsive to the needs of the individual and the organization.

Courage is identified as an essential component because most marginally performing managers remain in their positions, not because their inadequacies are unknown, but because their supervisors lack the mettle to take action. Otherwise capable, these leaders may be apprehensive about the institution's informal power structure, feel overextended, and be concerned about the time and effort associated with recruiting a more qualified replacement. Regrettably, they do a great disservice to their organization when they do not demonstrate the courage of their convictions, forcing others to pay a high price for their own timidity.

The term *compassion* is self-explanatory. However, genuine compassion in coping with the unavoidable discomfort associated with discharging a manager or any employee requires empathy for all the participants. Disbelief, anger, recrimination, bargaining, depression, and a host of other emotional reactions should be anticipated. Dealing with managers who have lied, cheated, violated the organization's policies, or committed some other unacceptable act is relatively easy compared with contending with managers who are simply not capable of performing their job despite extensive continuing education, counseling, and other interventions.

Compassion is an important ingredient in a supportive process that allows managers to leave the organization with the least possible damage to their dignity and self-confidence.

As implied at the outset, a hesitancy to confront management incompetence is universal. Yet the serious ramifications of inaction in a healthcare organization, where the quality of patient care is potentially at risk, cannot be denied. Consequently, executives have a moral obligation to act decisively and, by their own behavior, demonstrate that just as exemplary performance will be properly rewarded, consistently poor performance is unacceptable.

Originally published in the November/December 2005 issue of *Healthcare Executive* magazine.

Discussion Questions

Because the problem of incompetent managers continues to compromise employees, organizations, and potentially patients, what ethically defensible steps could reduce the frequency with which this issue occurs?

Of the six components of the author's plan for proceeding with termination, select the four you believe are the most important and explain why.

Abuse of Power

Paul B. Hofmann, DrPH, LFACHE

As a hospital executive, I am dismayed when I see certain physicians and managers using their power to intimidate patients, families, and staff. What can I do to stop this unethical behavior and prevent it in the future?

Unfortunately, abuse of power is at least as prevalent, if not more so, in healthcare organizations as it is in other types of organizations. Furthermore, because potential consequences are far more severe than in other settings, abuse of power in a clinical facility is particularly objectionable and unacceptable.

Patients and their families are exceptionally vulnerable in a time of crisis. They are apprehensive, sometimes frightened, and often intimidated by the organization's sheer physical size and bureaucratic complexity. Physicians, still at the top of the power structure in many hospitals, generally have a great deal of formal and informal organizational and personal leverage. Therefore, some individuals in authority (physicians as well as other clinical staff) may speak and act inappropriately, but this behavior is tolerated because patients and families often feel too overwhelmed and powerless to voice their objections.

Similar problems occur when managers who have significant authority do not use it for the good of the organization and those it serves. Employees under their supervision can be compromised by their misuse of power, adversely affecting both morale and productivity. Like patients and their families, employees may feel helpless and hesitant to object to such behavior.

Examples of abuse of power include rudeness, profane language, promise breaking, deception, dishonesty, and sexual harassment. Less obvious forms of abuse of power tend to be subtle and therefore more insidious; these include arrogance, use of overly confusing jargon, and withholding of information.

Management and medical staff sometimes rationalize this sort of unprofessional conduct because they view it as unintentional and non-malicious. However, in addition to compromising its immediate victims, tolerating such behavior has several negative long-term consequences, such as encouraging the individual to continue this conduct, silently condoning the behavior and suggesting to others that they can behave in a similar manner with impunity, demoralizing those who become aware of the organization's tolerance, and adversely affecting the image and reputation of the organization.

A variety of action steps can be taken to mitigate the abuse of power. Among them are the following:

- Recognize the inadequacy of well-intentioned rhetoric, including organizational values statements unaccompanied by explicit programs to reinforce them.
- Develop and implement a code of conduct for management, staff, and physicians.
- Perform periodic ethics audits that include questions about abuse of power (see "Performing an Ethics Audit" in the November/December 1995 issue of *Healthcare Executive*).
- Prepare a casebook with descriptions of unacceptable behavior and constructive interventions and use it in management orientation and training sessions.
- Conduct educational programs to promote candid discussion of these issues.
- Establish and encourage the use of a "hotline" to report inappropriate conduct.

- Sanction improper behavior promptly.
- Encourage the referral of physician problems to the medical staff's physician advisory committee.
- Emphasize the importance of sensitivity to the values of patients, families, and staff in routine employee performance appraisals.

Regrettably, it is unlikely that you can totally prevent abuse of power, but constant vigilance and effective intervention can reduce its incidence. Most importantly, you cannot achieve this objective unless senior management and clinical leaders themselves demonstrate zero tolerance for insensitive and inappropriate behavior.

Originally published in the March/April 1999 issue of *Healthcare Executive* magazine.

Discussion Questions

Assuming you agree that abuse of power remains a serious ethical problem in healthcare, as in other fields, why do you believe more progress has not been achieved in reducing its prevalence?

Of the nine steps suggested by the author to mitigate the abuse of power, select the four you believe would be most effective, and explain why.

The Values of a Profession

Everett A. Johnson, PhD, LFACHE

In every profession, a set of values—be it formal or informal—guides the behavior of individuals as they carry out their primary duties. For example, the chief financial officer of a business is responsible for maintaining a financially solvent organization within an ethical context; in medicine, clinicians take an oath to "do no harm" to the patient.

Those who choose a career in healthcare management are in the unique position of committing themselves to the values of business and medicine. At their core, both professions are guided by a similar quest to deliver the highest quality care possible. Yet as the needs of today's healthcare organizations often exceed available resources, administrative and medical concerns may occasionally seem to conflict with one another.

Balancing administrative and medical values can become a serious dilemma for healthcare executives when difficult decisions must be made. This challenge may be further complicated by the competing expectations of the other constituents that a healthcare organization serves. In addition to the needs of physicians and patients that should be considered, the business community, government agencies, and social service organizations may also express varying—and at times, conflicting—expectations. In situations where decisions are viewed by different constituencies as a choice between values, how should healthcare executives proceed?

Perhaps the best way executives can address such situations is to examine their leadership style and the system of values that their style sets for the organization. Effective leaders create an environment in which the values of the organization and the field of healthcare management are clear. Thus, when executives are faced with decisions that the organization's key stakeholders view as a choice between values, the course of action will be judged as fair. Following are several ways healthcare executives can foster an environment that embodies the values of healthcare management.

- **Place trust in the decision-making abilities of staff.** The freedom to make decisions without fear of reprisal is a necessary characteristic for superior performance. Excellent patient care occurs when caregivers are free to make professional decisions. Healthcare executives have a duty to encourage creativity and develop decision-making skills among staff at all levels of the organization. This creates respect and encourages collaboration between leadership and staff as well as administrators and clinicians.
- **Take accountability for subordinates.** In large organizations with several hierarchical levels, staff may make decisions that senior-level leaders are unaware of for quite some time. When employees fail to make appropriate decisions, the responsibility for those actions ultimately falls upon the organization's leadership. To blame an associate and deny responsibility creates distrust throughout the organization.
- **Be visible to caregivers on a daily basis.** Letting a hectic schedule justify administering from one's office is shortsighted. Executives who do so must then rely on internal reporting systems to bring problems to the forefront. Because minor issues that are easily ignored can later become major problems, executives who are visible and available on an informal basis have an opportunity to

sense their staff's problems and to address those problems in a compassionate and timely manner.

- **Help staff gain perspective.** When hard choices must be faced, the healthcare organization's constituents need to understand how their opinions, values, and expectations affect the organization as a whole. To facilitate understanding, executives can place conflicts in a wider perspective by being objective and forthright in addressing issues and sharing information. On major issues, timidity to initiate discussion may cause confusion and decrease confidence in the organization's leaders.
- **Lead with a consistent style and focus.** Senior-level leaders must be predictable in their decision making and actions. Uncertainty will lead to distrust and possibly diminish staff performance.

Effective leadership also requires healthcare executives to think about the emotional needs of constituents and to respond with both concern and caring that mirrors these feelings. In weighing the outcomes of a decision, consider the following questions:

- Does the decision demonstrate an appreciation for patients and staff?
- Does it conform to acceptable conduct?
- Does it show solicitude and the ideals of caring?
- Does it demonstrate careful attention to the implications of the decision?
- Is it consistent with and does it reinforce the vision and mission of the organization?

The values demonstrated through an executive's leadership style send a clear signal—both internally and to the community—of the values held by the organization. When leaders strive to pursue excellence in a just and fair manner, the entire organization will be inspired to reach for outstanding performance.

Originally published in the March/April 2002 issue of *Healthcare Executive* magazine.

Discussion Questions

The author properly emphasizes the need for senior management to take accountability for the decisions of subordinates, but what steps can be taken to minimize the likelihood that their decisions will be inappropriate and to ensure the profession's values will be upheld?

Five questions are suggested as litmus tests for weighing the emotional needs of constituents in making a decision, including patients and staff. What other questions might be considered?

The Value of an Ethics Audit

Paul B. Hofmann, DrPH, LFACHE

LIKE MOST ORGANIZATIONS, WE have well-crafted vision, mission and values statements, but it is difficult to determine our compliance with these statements. Is there a tool or process that can help us take our ethical pulse?

An ethics audit is a practical and valuable tool to evaluate where the organization may be falling below its own standards and expectations. Such an audit involves a comprehensive review of policies, procedures and perceptions to determine consistency with the organization's vision, mission, and values. When conducted properly, it provides an excellent snapshot of the institution's ethical climate.

The audit helps identify real and perceived problems. Both types of problems must be recognized to address them effectively. However, similar to performing any survey, it creates expectations that the findings will be summarized and shared, and an action plan will be prepared and implemented to deal with deficiencies.

SYMPTOMS SUGGESTING THE NEED FOR AN AUDIT

Employees, physicians and even communities are aware when an organization's rhetoric does not match reality. To avoid professional hypocrisy, practices must not contradict the institution's proclamations. A number of factors may suggest that an ethics audit should be initiated. These factors include

- decline in patient, employee or physician satisfaction ratings;
- higher turnover rates;
- reduction in community support as evidenced by the number and size of donations, number of volunteers and average weekly hours, and attendance at sponsored programs/events;
- allegations of conflicts of interest; or
- increase in litigation against the institution.

Ironically, the most important of these is none of the above. Indeed, an ideal time to perform an ethics audit is when there is no crisis or compelling set of problems. Every organization can benefit by periodically evaluating its ethical behavior.

AHA ORGANIZATIONAL ETHICS INITIATIVE

Ten years ago, as a member of the American Hospital Association's Organizational Ethics Task Force, I suggested the development of an ethics audit. Working with the assistance of the Ethics Resource Center in Washington, D.C., the task force produced a six-part organizational assessment tool. The six parts, which remain relevant today, focus on the following:

- Part one focused on existing organizational materials and raised questions about written statements of ethical principles, codes of conduct and pertinent policies and procedures. For example, what procedures help assure compliance with ethical requirements?

- Part two dealt with training, publications, and formal processes. For example, what would an employee be expected to do if he or she became aware of unethical activity and what steps would the organization take in responding to the report?
- Part three inquired about organizational structure. For example, if an ethics committee exists, what is its role in organizational ethics?
- Part four raised questions about organizational character. For example, what are the institution's ethical obligations to its community?
- Part five elicited the most significant ethical challenges facing the organization; respondents to a questionnaire were asked to rank, in order of priority, 24 potential issues.
- Part six was a survey that asked employees to assess the organization's ethics standards and practices; staff members were asked to indicate their degree of agreement or disagreement with 55 statements.

CONDUCTING AN ETHICS AUDIT AND BENEFITING FROM ITS RESULTS

As noted previously, an ethics audit should not be undertaken unless management is genuinely interested in sharing and addressing the findings. Once the commitment has been confirmed, a plan should be developed that provides a specific timeline for each component. These components include preparing a communication strategy to inform the organization and its stakeholders of the audit; collecting and analyzing appropriate documents; reviewing roles and responsibilities of key staff members and relevant committees; preparing interview and survey documents; performing the interviews and conducting the surveys; determining where there are contradictions and inconsistencies; and compiling and disseminating the results.

Of course, now comes the most critical step—after a complete diagnostic picture has been taken, detailed plans must be developed to address problem areas. Such plans might include redesigning interview and employment procedures. For instance, some employers ask about an applicant's values, describe those of the organization, and obtain a commitment from the applicant to support them.

Other steps could involve redesigning orientation and in-service education programs; establishing new policies, positions or committees; revising existing position descriptions or committee responsibilities; creating a casebook on ethical dilemmas for use in supervisory training to assist them in recognizing and reconciling competing values; implementing a telephone hotline to report questionable conduct; expanding the role of the institution's ethics committee to cover issues relating to both organizational and clinical ethics; and re-emphasizing compliance with the organization's code of conduct during performance reviews.

An ethics audit can be a powerful tool to acquire fresh insights about any major business. In a healthcare setting, if undertaken carefully, the ultimate beneficiaries should be patients and their families as well as the organization itself.

Originally published in the March/April 2006 issue of *Healthcare Executive* magazine.

Discussion Questions

Of the six parts identified as part of an ethics audit, which two do you believe are the most important, and why?

Similarly, of the various steps recommended after completion of an ethics audit, choose three you think are critical and explain your reasoning.

Selected Bibliography

Adelman, J. 2019. "High-Reliability Healthcare: Building Safer Systems Through Just Culture and Technology." *Journal of Healthcare Management* 64 (3): 137–41.

Agee, N. 2020. "Leadership in Disruptive Times: The Key to Changing Healthcare." *Frontiers of Health Services Management* 36 (3): 3–11.

Boyle, P., E. DuBose, S. Ellingson, D. Guinn, and D. McCurdy. 2001. *Organizational Ethics in Health Care: Principles, Cases, and Practical Solutions.* San Francisco: Jossey-Bass.

Brien, A. 1996. "Regulating Virtue: Formulating, Engendering and Enforcing Corporate Ethics Codes." *Business and Professional Ethics Journal* 15 (1): 21–52.

Brett, A., J. Raymond, D. Saunders, and G. Khushf. 1998. "An Ethics Discussion Series for Hospital Administrators." *Healthcare Ethics Committee Forum* 10 (20).

Collins, J. 2001. "Level 5 Leadership: The Triumph of Humility and Fierce Resolve." *Harvard Business Review* 79 (1): 66–76.

Daniels, N., and J. E. Sabin. 2008. *Setting Limits Fairly: Learning to Share Resources for Health*, 2nd ed. New York: Oxford University Press.

Darr, K. 2019. *Ethics in Health Services Management*, 6th ed. Baltimore, MD: Health Professions Press.

DeGeorge, R. 2009. *Business Ethics*, 7th ed. Upper Saddle River, NJ: Prentice Hall.

Dye, C. F. 2000. *Leadership in Healthcare: Values at the Top*. Chicago: Health Administration Press.

Emanuel, L. 2000. "Ethics and the Structures of Healthcare." *Cambridge Quarterly of Healthcare Ethics* 9 (2): 151–68.

Evans, M., L. Rosenbaum, D. Malina, S. Morrissey, and E. Rubin. 2020. "Diagnosing and Treating Systemic Racism." *New England Journal of Medicine* 383: 274–76.

Filerman, G., A. Mills, and P. Schyve (eds.). 2007. *Managerial Ethics in Healthcare: A New Perspective*. Chicago: Health Administration Press.

French, P. 1979. "The Corporation as a Moral Person." *American Philosophical Quarterly* 3: 207–15.

Friedman, E. 1996. *The Right Thing: Ten Years of Ethics Columns from the Healthcare Forum Journal*. San Francisco: Jossey-Bass.

Gilbert, J. 2007. *Strengthening Ethical Wisdom: Tools for Transforming Your Health Care Organization*. Chicago: Health Forum.

Goodstein, J., and R. L. Potter. 1999. "Beyond Financial Incentives: Organizational Ethics and Organizational Integrity." *Healthcare Ethics Committee Forum* 11 (4): 288–92.

Hall, R. T. 2000. *An Introduction to Healthcare Organizational Ethics*. New York: Oxford University Press.

Hiller, M. 1986. *Ethics and Health Administration: Ethical Decision Making in Health Management*. Arlington, TX: Association of University Programs in Health Administration.

Hofmann, P., and F. Perry (eds.). 2005. *Management Mistakes in Healthcare: Identification, Correction, and Prevention.* Cambridge: Cambridge University Press.

Jennings, B., B. H. Gray, V. A. Sharpe, L. Weiss, and A. R. Fleischman. 2002. "Ethics and Trusteeship for Health Care: Hospital Board Service in Turbulent Times." *Hastings Center Report Special Supplement* 32 (4): S1–S28.

Lahey, T., J. Pepe, and W. A. Nelson. 2017. "Principles of Ethical Leadership Illustrated by Institutional Management of Prion Contamination of Neurosurgical Instruments." *Cambridge Quarterly for Healthcare Ethics* 26: 173–79.

Lahey, T., and W. A. Nelson. 2020. "A Dashboard to Improve the Alignment of Healthcare Organization Decision-Making to Core Values and Mission Statement." *Cambridge Quarterly of Healthcare Ethics* 29 (1): 156–62.

Levey, S., and J. Hill. 1986. "Between Survival and Social Responsibility: In Search of an Ethical Balance." *Journal of Health Administration Education* 4 (2): 225–31.

Lown, B., A. Shin, and R. Jones. 2019. "Can Organizational Leaders Sustain Compassionate, Patient-Centered Care and Mitigate Burnout?" *Journal of Healthcare Management* 64 (6): 398–412.

Messick, D., and M. Bazerman. 1996. "Ethical Leadership and the Psychology of Decision Making." *Sloan Management Review* 37 (2): 9–22.

Morrison, E. 2006. *Ethics in Health Administration: A Practical Approach for Decision Makers.* Sudbury, MA: Jones and Bartlett Publishers.

Nash, L. 1990. *Good Intentions Aside: A Manager's Guide to Resolving Ethical Problems.* Boston: Harvard Business School Press.

Nelson, W. A. 2013. "The Imperative of a Moral Compass–Driven Healthcare Organization." *Frontiers of Health Services Management* 29 (1): 39–45.

Nelson, W. A., and J. Donnellan. "An Executive-Driven Ethical Culture." 2009. *Healthcare Executive* 24 (6): 44–46.

Nelson, W. A., R. C. Forcino, and G. Elwyn. 2017. "Patient-Centered Organizational Statements: Merely Rhetoric? A Survey of Health Care Leaders." *Health Care Manager* 36 (4): 1–5.

Nelson, W. A., and P. Hofmann (eds.). 2010. *Managing Healthcare Ethically: An Executive's Guide*, 2nd ed. Chicago: Health Administration Press.

Nelson, W. A., E. Taylor, and T. Walsh. 2014. "Building an Ethical Organizational Culture." *Health Care Manager* 33 (2): 158–64.

Ozar, D., J. Berg, P. Werhane, and L. Emanuel. 2001. "Organizational Ethics in Health Care: Toward a Model for Ethical Decision Making by Provider Organizations." *Institute for Ethics National Working Group Report*. American Medical Association.

Patel, M. 2020. "Navigating Unprecedented Change Through Agile and Disruptive Leadership." *Frontiers of Health Services Management* 36 (3): 34–39.

Pearson, S. D., J. E. Sabin, and E. Emanuel. 2003. *No Margin, No Mission: Health Care Organizations and the Quest for Ethical Excellence*. New York: Oxford University Press.

Perry, F. 2020. *The Tracks We Leave: Ethics in Healthcare Management*, 3rd ed. Chicago: Health Administration Press.

Prottas, D., and M. Nummelin. 2018. "Behavioral Integrity, Engagement, Organizational Citizenship Behavior, and

Service Quality in a Healthcare Setting." *Journal of Healthcare Management* 63 (6): 410–24.

Reiser, S. 1994. "The Ethical Life of Health Care Organizations." *Hastings Center Report* 24 (6): 28–35.

Ritvo, R. A., J. D. Ohlsen, and T. P. Holland. 2004. *Ethical Governance in Health Care: A Board Leadership Guide for Building an Ethical Culture*. Chicago: American Hospital Association.

Rorty, M. V., P. Werhane, and A. Mills. 2004. "The Rashomon Effect: Organization Ethics in Health Care." *HEC Forum* 16 (2): 75–94.

Seely, C., and S. Goldberger. 1999. "Integrated Ethics: Synecdoche in Healthcare." *Journal of Clinical Ethics* 10 (3): 202–209.

Spencer, E., and A. Mills. 1999. "Ethics in Healthcare Organizations." *Healthcare Ethics Committee Forum* 11 (4): 345–57.

Spencer, E., A. Mills, M. Rorty, and P. Werhane. 2000. *Organization Ethics in Health Care.* New York: Oxford Press.

Swensen, S., and T. Shanafelt. 2020. *Mayo Clinic Strategies to Reduce Burnout: 12 Actions to Create the Ideal Workplace.* Oxford, UK: Oxford University Press.

Tavistock Group. 1999. "A Shared Statement of Ethical Principles for Those Who Shape and Give Health Care." *Annals of Internal Medicine* 130 (2): 144–47.

Taylor, C. 2001. "The Buck Stops Here." *Health Progress* 82 (5): 37–47.

Trevino, L., M. Brown, and L. Hartman. 2003. "A Qualitative Investigation of Perceived Executive Ethical Leadership: Perceptions from Inside and Outside the Executive Suite." *Human Relations* 56 (1): 5–37.

Tuohey, J. 1998. "Covenant Model of Corporate Compliance." *Health Progress* 79 (4): 70–75.

Walshe, K., and S. Shortell. 2004. "When Things Go Wrong: How Health Care Organizations Deal With Major Failures." *Health Affairs* 23 (3): 103–11.

Weber, L. 2001. *Business Ethics in Healthcare: Beyond Compliance.* Indianapolis: Indiana University Press.

Werhane, P. 1990. "The Ethics of Health Care as a Business." *Business & Professional Ethics Journal* 9 (3 and 4): 7–20.

Woods, E. 2019. "The Mission Is the Message: Finding Hope and Common Ground in the Drive Toward Equity of Care." *Journal of Healthcare Management*. 64 (1): 6–9.

Woodstock Theological Center. 1995. *Ethical Considerations in the Business Aspects of Health Care.* Washington, DC: Georgetown University Press.

Worthley, J. A. 1997. *The Ethics of the Ordinary in Healthcare: Concepts and Cases.* Chicago: Health Administration Press.

About the Editors

William A. Nelson, PhD, MDiv, HFACHE, is director of the Ethics and Human Values Program and a professor in the Dartmouth Institute for Health Policy and Clinical Practice, the Department of Medical Education and the Department of Community and Family Medicine at Dartmouth's Geisel School of Medicine. He serves as the director of multiple courses for Dartmouth's three master of public health programs and medical school, focusing on healthcare ethics. He also is an adjunct professor at New York University's Robert F. Wagner Graduate School of Public Service.

From 1986 to 1989, Dr. Nelson was a W.K. Kellogg National Leadership Fellow, studying US and international healthcare policy. In 2008–2009, he was a National Rural Health Association Leadership Fellow. He is the author of more than 125 articles and many book chapters, and the editor of several books including the *Handbook for Rural Health Care Ethics*. He was the principal investigator of several federally and state-funded research studies fostering an evidence-based approach to ethics.

Dr. Nelson has received many awards, including the US Congressional Excalibur Award for Public Service and an honorary doctorate of humane letters from his alma mater, Elmhurst College. In 2013, he was named an Honorary Fellow of the American College of Healthcare Executives (ACHE) for "his pioneering work in healthcare organization ethics." He has received the Dartmouth Institute for Health Policy and Clinical Practice's student teaching award and, in 2018, was elected to the Geisel School of Medicine's Academy of Master Educators. In 2004, the US Department of Veterans Affairs established the annual competitive William A. Nelson Award for Excellence in Health Care Ethics. He has served as the ethics adviser to ACHE's Ethics Committee since 2006.

Paul B. Hofmann, DrPH, LFACHE, is president of the Hofmann Healthcare Group in Moraga, California. Although he devotes a majority of his time to pro bono activities, he continues to write, speak and consult on ethical issues in healthcare and to serve as an adviser to healthcare companies and as an expert witness.

Dr. Hofmann has served as executive director of Emory University Hospital and director of Stanford University Hospital and Clinics. For 19 years, he coordinated the annual two-day ethics seminar for the American College of Healthcare Executives (ACHE). He is coeditor of *Management Mistakes in Healthcare: Identification, Correction and Prevention*, published in 2005 by Cambridge University Press. He serves on the American Hospital Association's Quest for Quality Prize committee, the Joint Commission's international Standards Advisory Panel and the board of trustees of the Education Development Center. He is a cofounder of Operation Access and the Alliance for Global Clinical Training.

In 1976, Dr. Hofmann was the recipient of ACHE's Robert S. Hudgens Memorial Award for Young Hospital Administrator of the Year. In 2004, he received the Distinguished Leadership Award from the University of California Graduate Program in Health Management Alumni Association. He received the 2009 American Hospital Association's Award of Honor for his central role in shaping the understanding of healthcare ethics. In 2012, he was one of eight recipients of the national Schweitzer Leadership Award.

An author of more than 200 publications, Dr. Hofmann has held faculty appointments at Harvard, UCLA, Stanford, Emory, Seton Hall, and the University of California. His bachelor of science, master of public health, and doctor of public health degrees are from the University of California.

About the Contributors

Richard A. Culbertson, PhD, MHA, MDiv, is professor and director of health policy and systems management at the Louisiana State University (LSU) School of Public Health in New Orleans, professor of family medicine at LSU and a faculty associate of the American College of Healthcare Executives.

John J. Donnellan Jr., FACHE, is an adjunct professor of health policy and management at New York University's Robert F. Wagner Graduate School of Public Service.

Paul B. Gardent, MBA, CPA, is a clinical professor of business administration in the Tuck School of Business at Dartmouth College and an adjunct professor of health policy and clinical practice at The Dartmouth Institute for Health Policy and Clinical Practice.

Sinde A. Hahn, FACHE, CAE, is a retired senior vice president in the Department of Member Services at the American College of Healthcare Executives.

Raina H. Jain, MD, is a senior medical student at the Geisel School of Medicine at Dartmouth and will soon be training in internal medicine at NewYork-Presbyterian/Weill Cornell Medical Center.

Everett A. Johnson, PhD, LFACHE, served as the director of the Institute of Health Administration at Georgia State University.

Frankie Perry, RN, MA, LFACHE, is a former executive vice president of the American College of Healthcare Executives and currently serves on the faculty of the University of New Mexico.

Lauren A. Taylor, PhD, MDiv, MPH, is an assistant professor in the Department of Population Health at New York University's Grossman School of Medicine.

Eric Wadsworth, PhD, is an assistant professor at The Dartmouth Institute for Health Policy and Clinical Practice in the Geisel School of Medicine at Dartmouth.

Thom Walsh, PhD, is an associate professor of community medicine at the Oxley College of Health Sciences at the University of Tulsa and an adjunct professor at the Dartmouth Institute for Health Policy and Clinical Practice.